Honest Simplicity in William Carlos Williams'
"Asphodel, That Greeny Flower"

Of asphodel, that greeney flower,

that is a simple flower

like a buttercup upon its

branching stem, save ~~~~~~~~~

~~~~~~~ green and wooden -

We've had a long life

~~~~~~~ ~~~~ ~~~~~~~~~ ~~ ~~.

There are flowers also

in hell. ~~~~ Today I've come

to talk to you about ~~~~ ~~ flowers

that we both loved

even of this poor

colorless thing/that no one living

prizes

but the dead see and ask -

among themselves,

What do we remember that was shaped

as this thing

is shaped? as ~~~~~ eyes fill

with tears.

Of love, abiding love

it ~~~~~ be speaking.

~~~ too weak a wash of crimson

colors it.

Do you remember . . ?

Worksheet for Williams' "Asphodel, That Greeny Flower." Collection of American Literature, The Beinecke Rare Book and Manuscript Library, Yale University.

MARILYN KALLET

Honest Simplicity in William Carlos Williams' "Asphodel, That Greeny Flower"

LOUISIANA STATE UNIVERSITY PRESS
Baton Rouge and London

The author gratefully acknowledges permission to reprint excerpts from the following works of William Carlos Williams: *The Collected Earlier Poems of William Carlos Williams,* Copyright © 1938 by New Directions Publishing Corporation; *Interviews with William Carlos Williams,* Copyright © 1976 by the Estate of William Carlos Williams; *Many Loves,* Copyright © 1936, 1942, 1948 by William Carlos Williams; *Paterson,* Copyright © 1946, 1948, 1949, 1951, 1958 by William Carlos Williams; *Pictures from Breughel,* Copyright © 1949, 1951, 1952, 1954, 1955, 1956, 1957, 1959, 1960, 1961, 1962 by William Carlos Williams; *Selected Essays,* Copyright © 1954 by William Carlos Williams; Unpublished material by William Carlos Williams, Copyright © 1985 by William Eric Williams and Paul H. Williams. All of the above reprinted by permission of New Directions Publishing Corporation, agents. Quotations from the Williams holdings at the University at Buffalo are cited also with the permission of The Poetry/Rare Books Collection of the University Libraries, State University of New York at Buffalo. Quotations from the Williams holdings at Yale University are cited also with the permission of the Collection of American Literature, The Beinecke Rare Book and Manuscript Library, New Haven, Connecticut.

Grateful acknowledgment is also made to Edward Field for permission to use his translation of "Magic Words (After Nalungiaq)," in *Eskimo Songs and Stories,* selected and translated by Edward Field (Delacorte Press/Seymour Lawrence, 1973), and to Carroll F. Terrell for permission to use "Conversation as Design," in Carroll F. Terrell (ed.), *William Carlos Williams: Man and Poet* (Orono, Me., 1983), 323–42, which appears in slightly different form as Chapter 3 herein.

LIBRARY OF CONGRESS CATALOGING IN PUBLICATION DATA

Kallet, Marilyn, 1946–
  Honest simplicity in William Carlos Williams'
"Asphodel, that greeny flower".

  Includes index.
  1. Williams, William Carlos, 1883–1963. Asphodel, that greeny flower. I. Title.
PS3545.I544A934 1985   811'.52   84-25007
ISBN 0-8071-1226-7

Contents

Acknowledgments

I am grateful to Neil Baldwin and to Paul Mariani for their Williams scholarship, for their suggestions concerning my work, and for their encouragement. James Laughlin facilitated each stage of this work with his interest and his efficiency in providing whatever information or permissions were necessary.

Paul Williams, the elder son of William Carlos Williams, was kind enough to talk with me and to correspond. It was he who chose "Asphodel" as part of Flossie Williams' elegy in May, 1976. As he explained in a letter (December 13, 1983): "I selected 'Asphodel' to be read at Mom's funeral because I thought it was a beautiful poem about a beautiful woman—Mom."

Among friends who read the manuscript and provided both editorial comments and encouragement are Julia Demmin, Louis Gross, Deborah Harper, Steven Kallet, Martha Ostheimer, and Margaret Woodruff. I am grateful to them all.

David Schoonover, curator of the American Literature Collection at the Beinecke Rare Book Library, Yale University, facilitated my research and helped to make this work a pleasure. For assistance with other archival materials I am grateful to Gladys Eckardt, director, Rutherford Free Public Library; Eric Carpenter, and now Robert Bertholf, curators of the Poetry/Rare Books Collection, University Libraries, State University of New York at Buffalo; and Ellen Dunlap and Cathy Henderson, former and current Research Librarians at the Harry Ransom Humanities Research Center, The University of Texas at Austin. I am grateful also to the staff at Sweet Briar College Library for aiding me in my research.

I received research grants from Hobart & William Smith Colleges, and from the Hodges Fund of the English Department, The University of Tennessee, Knoxville. I wish to thank both sources. The Virginia Center for the Creative Arts in Sweet Briar, Virginia, provided me with a Residency in Winter, 1982, during which time I was able to work uninterruptedly on this book.

Finally, I would like to thank Beverly Jarrett at Louisiana State University Press for her patience, for excellent critical suggestions, and for her passionate interest in the work of William Carlos Williams.

Abbreviations

The following abbreviations of book titles are used throughout the footnotes. All works are by William Carlos Williams.

A	*The Autobiography of William Carlos Williams*. New York: New Directions, 1967.
CEP	*The Collected Earlier Poems*. New York: New Directions, 1966.
CLP	*The Collected Later Poems*. New York: New Directions, 1967.
ELG	"An Essay on Leaves of Grass," *Leaves of Grass: One Hundred Years After*, ed. Hindus. Stanford: Stanford University Press, 1955.
I	*Imaginations*. New York: New Directions, 1971.
Int	*Interviews with William Carlos Williams: "Speaking Straight Ahead."* New York: New Directions, 1976.
K	*Kora in Hell: Improvisations*. San Francisco: City Lights Books, 1967; original edition, London: Four Seas, 1920.
IWWP	*I Wanted to Write a Poem*. Boston: Beacon Press, 1958.
P	*Paterson*. New York: New Directions, 1963.

PB   *Pictures from Brueghel.* New York: New Directions, 1962.

SE   *The Selected Essays of William Carlos Williams.* New York: New Directions, 1954.

SL   *The Selected Letters of William Carlos Williams.* New York: McDowell, Oblensky, 1957.

UB   The Poetry/Rare Books Collection of the University Libraries, State University of New York at Buffalo.

HRHRC   The Harry Ransom Humanities Research Center, The University of Texas at Austin.

YALC   Yale Collection of American Literature, the Beinecke Rare Book and Manuscript Library, Yale University, New Haven, Connecticut.

Honest Simplicity in William Carlos Williams'
"Asphodel, That Greeny Flower"

Simplicity Where everything becomes simple is the most desirable place to be. But, like Wittgenstein and his "harmless contradiction," you have to remember how you got there. The simplicity must contain the memory of how hard it was to achieve. (The relevant Wittgenstein quotation is from the posthumously published "Remarks on the Foundations of Mathematics": "The pernicious thing is not to produce a contradiction in the region where neither the consistent nor the contradictory proposition has any kind of work to do; no, what *is* pernicious is: not to know how one reached the place where contradiction no longer does any harm.")

—Cornelius Cardew, "Virtues That a Musician Can Develop," *I-Kon*, 1968

Introduction

William Carlos Williams' long poem "Asphodel, That Greeny Flower" is beautiful in itself, without "irritable reaching after fact"; it sings of love, time, death, art, and the life of the imagination—crucial themes which the poet treats with tenderness and courage.[1] By acknowledging the work leading to the poem, by listening to the echoes of a lifetime of struggle that shuttle through the lines while the poem's music rises above struggle, the reader can appreciate the complex simplicity of "Asphodel" all the more. The apparent ease and gracefulness of the poem are the more striking when we are alert to obstacles the poet had to overcome. "Asphodel" was especially hard won; Williams worked all his life to reach the ease of tone, to achieve the metrical skill that makes the poem sing so fluently; he struggled also to affirm his love for his wife, Flossie. The poem reaches into the depths of Williams' being for this assertion of love, which is also a defiance of speechlessness, of dying "incommunicado." Set last among the late poems that Williams called *Journey to Love* (1955), "Asphodel" contains the memory of how hard it was to get there, to the "desirable place" in poetry and personal feelings where "contradiction no longer does any harm."

1. *PB*, 153–82. "Asphodel" was first published in its entirety in *Journey to Love* (New York, 1955).

Williams' fifty years of work at craft are buttressed with theoretical work and reflections on "measure"; for most of his life the poet sought in a disciplined way to mark out the rhythm of a new American verse. The new lines must be cut with mathematical precision, for what is at stake is the life of the mind, the imagination captured in its time and locale as "the radiant gist," the "common language" of poetry.[2] Williams listened for the sound and rhythm in the speech patterns of the American language that would reveal our experiences to us. Music hovers in our distinctive landscapes, stirring the poet to his work.

> A music
> supersedes his composure, hallooing to us
> across a great distance . .
>   wakens the dance
> who blows upon his benumbed fingers!
> ("The Desert Music," *PB*, 109)

The poet's fingers were literally "benumbed"—Williams had suffered his first stroke in March, 1951, and composed "The Desert Music" shortly thereafter. The poem sings "a music of survival," as the words reawaken the poet's faith in his resources. The poems in *The Desert Music* and *Journey to Love* are songs of healing as well as love songs, whose lines restore the aging poet and his world with an affirmation of creative powers.[3] "Asphodel," written for the most part after the poet had suffered a second debilitating stroke in August, 1952, also invokes reintegration and healing. The poet writes to save his marriage, his sanity, and his life, though the urgency of "Asphodel" is tempered by the triadic line, a measure that unfolds gradually.

The theme of music, of a design that transcends the "sorry facts" of existence, recurs in the late poems. In "The Or-

2. *P*, 133, 218. Adrienne Rich writes of *The Dream of a Common Language* (New York, 1978). Williams also sings of community, of poet-companions who "have come a long way, commonly" (*P*, 269).
3. William Carlos Williams, *The Desert Music* (New York, 1954). All the poems from this volume appear in *PB*; "Work in Progress" becomes the first section of "Asphodel" in the *Journey to Love* chapter of *PB*.

chestra," music, design, poetry, and love all become interchangeable.

> Now is the time .
> > in spite of the "wrong note"
> > > I love you. My heart is
>
> innocent.
> > And this the first
> > > (and last) day of the world
>
> The birds twitter now anew
> > but a design
> > > surmounts their twittering.
>
> It is a design of a man
> > that makes them twitter.
> > > It is a design. (*PB*, 82)

In this address to his wife Williams posits a genesis and a simultaneous acknowledgment of farewell; everything is at stake in the quality of his song, and of his love. The natural world—seen anew this time at a distance from its hectic activity—is made musical by the achievement of the poem's design. The poem remembers the world it has lived through, with its wrong notes and twitterings, even as the music surmounts it.

Williams never shunned the "out of tune" in his work. In his view, all the subjects of daily life might be treated imaginatively in the poem. He did not believe in the "anti-poetic," though traditionalists might have thought they found it in his work. A growing consciousness of his own frailty, brought on by illness and age, pervades the late poetry; the poems—"in tune" by now—defy this inevitable frailty with the beauty and vigor of their design.

"Music" in the late poems refers not only to the sound effects of the poems, to "heard melodies," but to the impact of the poems, to the unique integrative quality of verse that allows poetry to transcend the "twittering" or creaking of its machinery. If "love and the imagination / are of a piece," so are music and the imagination, or music and love. The great themes that Williams embraces in "Asphodel"—love, time, destruction, and the powers of the imagination—are held together by the poem's music, its sound, lines, and resounding images. Williams' use of his special tercet, the triadic line with its variable foot, creates a pleasing effect to the ear.

> Of asphodel, that greeny flower,
>   like a buttercup
>   upon its branching stem—
> save that it's green and wooden—
>   I come, my sweet,
>   to sing to you. (PB, 153)

Here is an epithalamion, a stately air, lightened by its directness and by the syncopation of the three-ply line. The music of Williams' late poetry, its actual sound, conveys a sense of timelessness and continuity not found in most of the earlier works, however daring those poems are. Breaking ground makes noise. An atmosphere of quiet begins subtly to permeate the late poems, intermingling through the spaces created by the triadic lines with the music of the lines. A "desirable place to be," aesthetically.

"Asphodel," written in 1952–1953, published in 1955 when the poet was seventy-two years old, is, in its sureness of form and richness of content, a summation of Williams' work at life and craft. The poem is no longer pure improvisation such as we find in Kora in Hell: Improvisations (1920), a collection of surrealistic exercises attentive to the fleeting passages of the poet's life, notes stolen away from the time Williams spent at his medical practice. "Asphodel" is the result of a lifetime of traveling in unknown, uncharted metrical seas, the lyrical place discovered as the result of sustained willingness to improvise in a disciplined manner. Williams dedicated Kora to Flossie, yet she is buried there in Williams' mysterious and obscure prose; we find her mainly in the poet's painful recognition of his discontentment. "I confess I wish my wife younger. This is the lewdest thought possible: it makes a mockery of the spirit, say you? . . . I wish for youth! I wish for love—!" Life and art miss each other; the poet turns from his wife to poetry: "Knowing she will never understand his excitement he consoles himself with the thought of art" (K, 48, 67).

The discovery of "love, abiding love" and of clarity of form comes only after many years of marriage and of work at craft.

Uncertainties did not deter the poet from starting out: Williams enjoyed the momentum of traveling, exploring; at times the lines might lead unexpectedly to a desirable image.

> Why bother where I went?
> for I went spinning on the
>
> four wheels of my car
> along the wet road until
>
> I saw a girl with one leg
> over the rail of a balcony (*CEP*, 259)

Outside the poem, Williams' love of traveling toward women may have gotten him into trouble with Flossie. "Asphodel" sings a confession, an explanation of sorts, through its return home.

As a physician, Williams spent time in the car traveling hurriedly from place to place; he used the experience of being on the road as a theme for some poems; the kinetics of his lines reflect the poet's delight in pure movement. Driving can also offer a more leisurely kind of traveling, a "purposiveness without purpose," that leads on one journey not to a precipice, but to a deep and secret place.

> I ride in my car
> I think about
>
> prehistoric caves
> in the Pyrenees—
>
> the cave of
> *Les Trois Frères* ("The Avenue of Poplars," *CEP*, 281)

In "Asphodel" Williams returns to the theme of images found in prehistoric caves; he goes deeper toward the sources of art. The worksheets for "Asphodel," the focus of the last chapter of this study, show how Williams explored different avenues or possibilities in his poem.[4] Even in the late poems "traveling" produces the unexpected; precipices and roadblocks must be avoided to get to the new destination.

4. "Paterson: Book V" (Worksheets, YALC).

Williams was especially gifted at taking risks in his work. He abandoned the safety of conventional British prosody as he worked toward the discovery of a new verse form. Within his lines he scorns those who stay in place, fearing risk. Too much depends upon imaginative work.

> . . . unless there is
> a new mind there cannot be a new
> line, the old will go on
> repeating itself with recurring
> deadliness . . . . (P, 65)

"Without invention" even the natural world deteriorates, "crumbled now to chalk." For most of his life Williams worked without formal certainty, until finally in Book Two of *Paterson* he arrived at the form that would serve him for *Journey to Love*. Williams had a special talent for waiting in formlessness as he wrote. He worked with the "clairvoyant conviction" that if not he, then some other poet still to come would find the new measure; he leaned forward imaginatively into this discovery, until he arrived at the "sea-change," the triadic line.[5]

In the process of writing or "traveling" in a state of awareness, one might even seek to produce contradictions, rather than to avoid them. "But why not e.g. in order to show that everything in the world is uncertain?" One might be "anxious to produce contradictions, say for aesthetic purposes."[6] Surely in *Kora in Hell*, where "imagination but delights in its own seasons reversing the usual order at will," contradictions are the order or disorder of the day. "Of the air of the coldest room" the imagination "will seem to build the hottest passions" (K, 15). *Kora* predicts the magical reversal of seasons that occurs in "Asphodel," where the sick and aging poet re-

5. Williams first uses the triadic line in *P*, 96. The reference to a "sea-change" is from Williams' *I Wanted to Write a Poem* (Boston, 1958), 83. In "Virtues that a Musician Can Develop" Cornelius Cardew praises the state of "clairvoyant conviction" ("Preparedness . . . or simply Awakeness") as important to the musician who improvises. *I-Kon*, I (1968), 19.
6. Ludvig Wittgenstein, *Remarks on the Foundations of Mathematics* (Cambridge, Mass., 1956), 105e, 106e.

creates the certainty of springtime for Flossie, loving her "always for the first time."

Those who seek out contradictions, as Williams did, may not find them practical or useful, but they "still would be glad to lead their lives in the neighborhood of a contradiction."[7] Contemporary poetry is a "neighborhood of contradictions"; Williams lived all his life in that neighborhood, from *Kora* to *Paterson*, until settling down there in the late poems. In "Asphodel" Williams has control over his contradictions: we hear the "stress and counterstress" of the powers of art and of the great discoverers pitted against the destructive powers of recent history: the bomb, the McCarthy "witch hunts," the senseless burning of priceless paintings and books instigated by Perón in Buenos Aires.[8] Yet in "Asphodel" creation triumphs, the contradictions of loving and not-loving (betrayal), of creation and destruction are "rendered harmless" by the poet's clarity of design and strength of feeling. "Asphodel" is Williams' great poem of reconciliation. At least, the poet hopes that he may render harmless the contradictions of his lifetime, by convincing Flossie of his late but good intentions.

"Asphodel" contains the memory of how hard it was to get there. Begun at a time when Williams was physically weak (March, 1952), worked on when he was virtually incapacitated and restricted to his memories (1953), the poem contains a sea of personal and literary memories to voyage on, a garden of specific images from boyhood and adult life, which, like pressed flowers, trigger again the awakening of creative life. Embedded in the poem is the structure of a descent myth as well. As Williams speaks of his journey to hell, we follow him in his memory down through the subway toward an elusive image of his father, down to the prehistoric artwork in caves. "Asphodel" has the depth charge of myth, the most profound and comprehensive kind of memory. While

---

7. *Ibid.*, 105e.
8. Williams probably read about the burning of paintings and of the library at the Buenos Aires Jockey Club in New York *Times*, April 16, 1953, Sec. 1, p. 4. See *PB*, 168.

the waves of the poem's lines glint on the surface, its deeper treasures wakened are more complex; the lines are no more the work of a child than the drawings on the walls at Lascaux, or the paintings of Paul Klee. The poem remembers how hard it has been for the poet and for human consciousness to come to creation in the face of personal struggles and brutal communal histories.

The poem is the flower that Williams had awaited blossoming in his imagination. "Asphodel" becomes a design for meditation. Throughout his literary career Williams gathered images of flowers for his poetry, among them Queen Anne's lace, locust flowers, the mustard flower, and finally, asphodel, violets, and roses. As in tribal poetry, praise poems like the Navajo "Night Chant," incantation collects the world.[9] Images gather like petals to the imaginative core, to the poet's final expression of self. Finally, the song, the flower, stands for the singer and his world. "Asphodel," the flower of local meadows and the mythic flower of Hades, crosses worlds, as do Yeats' dolphins. The poem is a preparation for death as well as a love song.

"Asphodel" contains its own memories, but there are also memories that we can bring to the poem to enrich a reading. A study of earned simplicity requires a look at contexts: how did Williams manage to write about a life redeemed by memory, about abiding love, at a time when imaginative freedom in America was being shut down? The early 1950s with its Cold War and persecution of intellectuals and artists had to be a difficult time in which to generate warmth. And though Williams thrived on risk, the suspiciousness and intellectual oppression generated in Washington caused him to suffer deeply.

Not everyone can use a journey to hell—in this case a physical and mental breakdown—as a source for poetry. Williams faced obstacles like his illnesses and his persecution by those in Washington by overcoming these personal hells in his po-

9. Margot Astrov (ed.), *The Winged Serpent: American Indian Prose and Poetry* (New York, 1962), 186.

etry. "Nothing is lost" on the poet. As a physician Williams had practiced healing all his life. Self-healing was part of his strength as an artist. The use of hell as a source of song and new life is a shamanic trick, the work of an Orphic poet.

"Asphodel" is a love poem to Flossie, and a poem of self-healing; it also represents a long-sought-after metrical accomplishment. Recognition of Williams' work on metrics helps us to appreciate measure in practice in the poem. "The notes for the poem are the only poem" says Adrienne Rich, emphasizing the process of writing.[10] Williams' theories and reflections on metrics have a substance and validity of their own, the way his poetry does.

In his biography of Williams, Paul Mariani has superbly covered the materials of Williams' life, imagining his existence for us with documentation from his writings.[11] Yet in reference to "Asphodel" we must acknowledge the poet's struggle toward the poem by reviewing certain details of biography and literary biography.

The text itself will tell us what we need to know about its beauty. How does the poet make his poem sound simple and direct? How does he translate the idea into the "thing," effecting his discovery of a new measure in "Asphodel"?

The surface of the text and an analysis of its unifying action, "to journey towards love," lead to the deeper structure of the poem, to its mythic pattern. Williams' descent into memory allows him to restore to Flossie an image of their wedding, an image charged with gratitude and light. "Asphodel" uses the past to create a timeless image. Williams restores the past through his poetry, as Proust did in his great novel, though the differences are striking. Though he uses memory as a source of renewal, Williams loves the *actual*—the present, and the future outside him.

The worksheets or rough drafts of "Asphodel" also represent a kind of descent: into the anarchic state of the creative

10. Adrienne Rich, *The Will to Change* (New York, 1971), 49.
11. Paul Mariani, *William Carlos Williams: A New World Naked* (New York, 1981).

process. Through a study of these worksheets we are privileged to see how carefully Williams worked on the poem, how lines are pared and revised for content to present us in their bareness with their wealth, "a thousand topics in an apple blossom," a world condensed into the "simple" asphodel.[12]

12. On p. 5 of a typed worksheet in the YALC marked "Paterson V (for Flossie)" Williams uses the phrase "a thousand tropics in an apple blossom"—also an evocative image. Another typed draft in YALC marked "(*for Flossie*)" with "a dialogue" penciled in speaks of asphodel "that is a simple flower."

Part I

LABOR TO BE
BEAUTIFUL

CHAPTER ONE

To Know Life

What pressed Williams throughout his life (1883–1963) to work so hard at verse, at doctoring, at seeking out the company of painters, poets, and "a field of women," finally at seeking Flossie's understanding? "I have told you before that my two leading forces were trying to know life and trying to find a technique of verse," Williams reiterates in a statement to Edith Heal (*IWWP*, 82–83). A master craftsman is speaking, whose life and work inform each other throughout the journey to skill and love. Particularly in his later years Williams' feelings, his memories and reflections, became a source for his poetry. "Asphodel" sings what Williams lived, and he relives through the music. The poem means to reach out to Flossie and to bring a message of renewed love and faith in art to its readers. Robert Lowell remembers the last time he heard Williams read, when the poet, half-paralyzed, recited "Asphodel" to a crowd of three thousand listeners at Wellesley College. "No one stirred. In the silence he read his great poem, 'Of Asphodel, That Greeny Flower,' a triumph of simple confession—somehow he delivered to us what was impossible, something that was both poetry and beyond poetry."[1] The poem had transformed itself back into life.

1. Robert Lowell, "William Carlos Williams," in J. Hillis Miller (ed.), *William Carlos Williams: A Collection of Critical Essays* (Englewood Cliffs, 1966), 159.

"Asphodel" is Williams' triumph over obstacles in his life and work. The poem refers explicitly and implicitly to his journey to hell, and to his struggle for renewal. Descent, chaos, struggle, were never ends for Williams, as he indicates in an early poem:

> From disorder (a chaos)
> order grows
> —grows fruitful.
> The chaos feeds it. Chaos
> feeds the tree. ("Descent," *CEP*, 460)

"The ascent beckoned" to creativity even as "the descent beckons" to an exploration of life's terrors. The music and the calm tone of "Asphodel" convey a joy that transcends the memory of struggle. In an early poem Williams predicts release through music: "As from an illness, as after drought / the streams released to flow . . . / So / after love a music streams above it" (*CEP*, 108). So after a lifetime of hard work, love and music become one.

"As from an illness," the poem releases an antitoxin, a working toward cure of the ills it presents. "It is the mind / the mind / that must be cured," Williams diagnoses in "Asphodel" (*PB*, 159). The early 1950s was a time of political and social illness in America, a difficult time "to know life," since who and what one knew were being monitored by the House Un-American Activities Committee. The presence of the bomb had become routine: "President Eisenhower told a recent visitor that he had been having atomic bombs for breakfast."[2] "Asphodel" reminds us of the destructive presence of the bomb, and of our fascination with its power.

> The mere picture
>   of the exploding bomb
> fascinates us
>   so that we cannot wait
>   to prostrate ourselves
> before it. (*PB*, 165)

2. *Life*, October 19, 1953, p. 38.

In May, 1952, "Atomic Open House" was held by the Atomic Energy Commission. Through the mass-circulation magazines, everyone was invited to see pictures of the explosions. A beautiful "rose-colored doughnut" appeared just before the spectacle of a mushroom-shaped cloud.[3] "We do not believe / that love / can so wreck our lives," or rebuild them, but in the face of such destructive possibilities Williams must remind us in the poem about love's powers (*PB*, 165).

Tempered by "what passes for the new," by those pictures of rosy doughnuts that pervaded the news in the 1950s, men and women lack sustenance; they "die miserably every day / for lack / of what is found there" (*PB*, 161–62). The poet's concern is to provide for himself and for us from a deeper imaginative life. Only by imagining our existence as fully as possible can we continue to survive. The poem is a different kind of flower, not slick, not deceptively beautiful, but rich with the truth of our lives, a working-through of the poet's experience of hurting, healing, and reparation through love. Williams' personal illness, his troubled physical condition and the trouble he had experienced in his marriage, lead the poet to think about the larger community, and to return him to the artist's responsibility for the quality of our lives.

The poet's responsibility is to not fall silent. Unlike most who "come to our deaths in silence," unlike the death he fears, the poet hopes to live and die singing. There is enough enforced silence to go around.

> The bomb speaks.
>   All suppressions,
> from the witchcraft trials at Salem
>   to the latest
>   book burnings
> are confessions
>   that the bomb
>   has entered our lives
> to destroy us. (*PB*, 168)

3. *Life*, May 26, 1952, pp. 49–52.

Against suppression Williams evokes tender personal memories in "Asphodel" that he has tucked away, pressed in a book for safekeeping. He summons the names of other artists and explorers, Villon, Rimbaud, René Char, Columbus, Darwin, in defense of imaginative daring. He offers all he can, his life-giving skills in opposition to the forces of history. As an obstetrician, he counts to his credit "some baby's life / which had been lost / had I not intervened" (*PB*, 169). "But the words" are most important, their impending loss most significant to Williams. Through words the poet has grown to make an imaginary place where he can greet his wife in old age.

> For in spite of it all,
>   all that I have brought on myself,
>   grew that single image
>   that I adore
>   equally with you
>   and so
>   it brought us together. (*PB*, 169)

Williams "regrets most" the end of his poetry, which will also be the end of his life. He "talks on against time" in "Asphodel," and like Shakespeare singing of "that time of year" he manages to be a wrestler, to hold his own in the music.

The calm and steady tone of "Asphodel" does not betray how personally Williams suffered from the witch hunts of the 1950s. McCarthyism drilled directly into his side, when, by accusation and innuendo he was kept from holding the position of Poetry Consultant at the Library of Congress. The offer had been extended by Robert Lowell in 1948, but by 1952, when Williams was ready to leave his medical practice and accept the job, he was told that he would have to await security clearance. A committee at the Library would evaluate the findings of an FBI investigation. Poems written years earlier ("Russia" and "The Pink Church") were cited by watchful citizens as evidence against him, as were his signatures (along with those of other noted intellectuals) in support of supposedly radical causes in the 1930s. Williams engaged his lawyer to fight for his reputation and his right to the job, but the struggle cost him dearly, helping to cause his serious depression. In February, 1953, Williams entered a private mental hospital in Queens, where he was treated by psychiatry. For the eight weeks of his stay he continued his own form of therapy in his poetry, in his letters to his wife.[4]

If Williams had not been ill to begin with, he might have weathered the Library of Congress affair more easily. But having just suffered a second stroke in the summer of 1952, experiencing partial paralysis, difficulty with his writing hand, his speech, and his eyes, Williams was battling his own sense of impotence. He was not in shape to take on the powers that were, though he did so anyway.

Yet Williams' patience, his "forebearance" or stubbornness, showed up in his attitude toward his illnesses as well as toward his work. The later poems (1951–1961) are a poetic history of response to illness, though there is no trace of self-pity in the poetry. There are no references in *Pictures from Brueghel* (1962) to specific illnesses, but rather to aging and mortality, to love, music, art, and the imagination. A heart attack in 1948 and the subsequent strokes that Williams suffered in the early 1950s challenged him to write some of his best verse.

"The Desert Music," a long poem of struggle and affirmation of Williams' identity as a poet, was his response to the first "superficial stroke" in 1951. Williams had just returned from a trip out West, to El Paso, when he suffered the stroke. He wrote "The Desert Music" in the aftermath of this shock to his system. An invitation to read his poetry at Harvard provided an impetus for him to ready the poem. "The Desert Music" is saturated with music—the music of the bars, of the noisy streets of El Paso, the music of an old whore doing her strip dance. But the poet is also listening within for the recovery of his poetic voice; the desert that Williams had faced was

4. See Paul Mariani, *William Carlos Williams: A New World Naked* (New York, 1981), 651–67 for a detailed account of Williams' problems with the Library of Congress appointment, and for a description of the aftermath.

his loss of creative power, and his death.[5] The poet expects through his writings to lift himself "up and out of terror, / Up from before the death living around" and living within him (*CEP*, 6). In his early poem "The Wanderer" (1914) the poet had been initiated, allowed by his old guide to "behold himself old" and then to feel his timelessness. In *The Desert Music* and in *Journey to Love* the old poet himself becomes the guide and rescuer, "reversing seasons at will," renewing himself and his love through the poem.

His first stroke must have provoked in Williams doubts about his artistry, for in "The Desert Music" he insists, "I *am* a poet! I / am. I am. I am a poet, I reaffirmed" (*PB*, 120). The music of contact with a formless shape, with a beggar huddled on a bridge in El Paso, reawakens Williams not only to the terror of formlessness but also to its promise. He faces his death and returns with an image, with an understanding that music wraps poetry in life, gives back a sense of birth to the writer even when he is old.

> . . . I stood aghast and looked at it—
> in the half-light: shapeless or rather returned
> to its original shape, armless, legless,
> headless, packed like the pit of a fruit into
> that obscure corner—or
> a fish to swim against the stream—or
> a child in the womb prepared to imitate life,
> warding its life against
> a birth of awful promise. The music
> guards it, a mucus, a film that surrounds it,
> a benumbing ink that stains the
> sea of our minds—to hold us off—shed
> of a shape close as it can get to no shape,
> a music! a protecting music   . (*PB*, 119–20)

The poems in *The Desert Music* and in *Journey to Love*, especially "Asphodel," are a "holding off" of death through the strength of the poem's measure.

5. See Sherman Paul, *The Music of Survival: The Biography of a Poem by William Carlos Williams* (Urbana, 1968), 16.

From his close touch with formlessness, with death, Williams returns with a new music. The rest of the poems in *The Desert Music* and in *Journey to Love* are written in the triadic line. "Chaos feeds the tree" with order. The theme of these two books is one, the renewal of life through memory and love, through the dance and music in the poet's lines.

A more severe stroke hit Williams in August, 1952, paralyzing him on his right side. "Asphodel," first conceived by Williams to be a part of *Paterson V*, begun in 1952, was typed mostly with the forefinger of his left hand. One has only to look at the worksheets for "Asphodel" to be moved by the drama of work on the poem. The scrawl of Williams' notes for the poem, his notes in the margins, show how difficult and painful it must have been for him to write at all. Yet that physical and emotional struggle has been removed from the printed poem, which "flows gently," not dwelling on impediments but deriving character, syncopation, from overcoming them.

Williams speaks directly in his letters about the effect of his illnesses. In June, 1952, he describes the literal hell of his condition in a letter to David McDowell. "This has been one hell of an illness, this nervous instability. . . . It saps your marrow, it really does. It's a terrific drain too on the forbearance of a devoted wife and friends. And God knows you need your friends. . . . A man fears everything in the world and out of it, in heaven and in hell. I tell you the poets are not dreamers; they know what they are and what they are talking about is a living hell" (*SL*, 314). The demons of "nervous instability" that Poe or Baudelaire must have feared were not alien to Williams, though his verse is more cheerful, more of the daylight world than theirs. When Williams is able to transpose his struggle into poetry, he, like Baudelaire, will speak of finding that there are "flowers also / in hell" (*PB*, 153).

"Death is the mother of beauty," for Williams, as for Stevens and other writers of skill and courage. His illnesses impressed on Williams how much work he still had to do, pushing him to integrate his experiences into his final compositions.

This is the second time I have been knocked out. But this time I seem to have come out of it with a clearer head. Perhaps it derived from a feeling that I might have died or, worse. . . . As a result of the enforced idleness and opportunity for thought, it may be, I have brought hard down on the facts of a situation which can no longer be delayed in the bringing of it to a final summary. I must now, in other words, make myself clear. I must gather together the stray ends of what I have been thinking and make my full statement as to their meaning or quit. (*SL*, 298)

The late poems, scrupulous in their formal leanness, resonate with the "final summary" Williams brings to them.

The reality of his declining physical powers, of his impending death, may have frightened Williams, but it did not leave him feeling hopeless for long. As he explained in *I Wanted to Write a Poem*, "*Paterson V* must be written. . . . Why must it be written? . . . it can't be categorically stated that death ends *anything*. When you're through with sex, with ambition, what can an old man create? Art, of course, a piece of art that will go beyond him . . ." (*IWWP*, 22). The poet of process and perception, who captures the moment's "scent," is also the poet whose imagination "feeds upon" those instants, hoping to create art's lasting memory. Williams states the artist's human goal in a forthright but lively manner:

> Come on!
> 'Do you want to live
> forever?—
> That
> is the essence
> of poetry. (*PB*, 139)

Even the contemporary poet, caught in the whirl of relativity, wants his work to hold on, wants the immortality of the bards; but his work "does not / always / take the same form." In its changes the form must be quick, pliable enough to capture what does not change. No more "gilded monuments"— the contemporary poem becomes a "dance figure."

"Love / combating sleep," Williams managed to continue work on "Asphodel" even in his lowest moments, during his stay at the mental hospital. While he must have been feeling imprisoned physically, oppressed by his own mental state, his poem sang freely, allowing him room to breathe. When he must have been feeling most isolated, his poem made the contact with Flossie that he needed to survive. Like his old friend Ezra Pound, who wrote his best poetry while imprisoned in a gorilla cage at Pisa, Williams had written some of his best, freest verse while feeling closed in. "Like amnesiacs / in a ward on fire, we must / find words / or burn" a young contemporary poet, Olga Broumas, sings; at times in a poet's or a community's life finding a language becomes survival.[6] Williams writes in *Paterson* about the "cost of dreams. / in which we search, after a surgery / of the wits and must translate, quickly / step by step or be destroyed . . ." (124). Williams speaks here of "risking life" as he writes; *Paterson's* serious metaphors for the poet's illness (the creative block, the loss of language), and the cure through art become a reality once more as Williams restores his balance, his happiness, through the articulate lines of "Asphodel."

In his letters to the young poet Denise Levertov, Williams had advised her to practice her writing continuously in the event a crisis should call for her full aesthetic powers: "At times there's nothing to do but finger exercises. Maybe that's the end. You do it merely to keep supple. For what dreadful encounter? Nothing may happen, I hope it never does—but if it does, your only chance of doing some arresting writing, something that the world is really waiting for with open arms, is to be ready."[7] The ominous tone in Williams' letter may be explained by the political climate of the 1950s, with the bomb always in the background. Or Williams' own recent experiences explain this tone: his skills built up over the years were there when he most needed them to communicate to Flossie and his readers.

6. Olga Broumas, *Beginning With O* (New Haven, 1977), 24.
7. William Carlos Williams, "Letters to Denise Levertov," *Stony Brook*, I/II (Post-Fall, 1968), 164.

The poems in *Journey to Love*, including "Asphodel," convey foremost a sense of commitment to the imagination. Without Williams' letters and the biographical information that we now have, we would not suspect that Williams had felt so tortured, imperiled; self-torture has been erased from the published works.[8] Upon reading "The Mental Hospital Garden" we might think that Williams had only gone there for a stroll. The late poems tell us that a "healing odor is abroad," and *that* is the scent we are to follow (*PB*, 97–100; 78).

For more than forty years he had been curing others, but in his later years Williams had to apply his imaginative skills to healing himself. His years of experience as a physician, working primarily as an obstetrician, bear on his success as a poet. His doctoring gave him the contact with people and with experience that nourished his writing. Though it is tempting to mythologize the poet, especially an obstetrician, as a midwife or "deliverer" of his poems, Williams did not romanticize himself as a shaman, or medicine man. For one thing, medicine kept him busy, kept him from writing. He worked at doctoring in order to make a living. "Nine tenths of the problem / is to live," Williams says in *Paterson*, and goes on to gently parody the townspeople who admire his "pastime" of writing poetry—without having an idea of what that work cost him (*P*, 138). Working at two full lives, at being both physician and poet, must have been exhausting and strengthening at the same time.

Though Williams sometimes wished he had a button to push to cure the sick, he also spoke of his work as a physician as part of what made his poetry successful. His persona in *Paterson* and in the *Autobiography* is that of the country doctor, both naïve and clever, amazed by the many dramas he witnessed and participated in. Doctoring gave Williams a passkey to enter into people's lives, to watch and, most importantly, to listen to their stories.

In retrospect, Williams described his medical career as an

8. *SL*, 298–329.

asset to his writing, a completion of his sense of work. Poetry is an extension of the concern for healing. In 1950 Williams said in an interview, "It was always important to me to go through the somatic part of medicine into the psychic part, which is verse, which is art, all the way through" (*Int*, 18). The poems in *Journey to Love*, including "Asphodel," attempt to heal the damage that may have been done to love through time and the poet's own cruelties.

In the chapter of his *Autobiography* called "The Practice," Williams speaks of being privileged to witness private dramas, deaths, births, gropings for life and speech. His compassion for those struggling to articulate pain inspired him all the more to capture the rhythms of speech in poetry. "Do we not see that we are inarticulate?" he asks.

> That is what defeats us. It is our inability to communicate to another how we are locked within ourselves, unable to say the simplest things of importance to one another. . . .
> The physician enjoys a wonderful opportunity actually to witness the words being born. Their actual colors and shapes are laid before him carrying their tiny burdens which he is privileged to take into his care. . . . He may see the difficulty with which they have been born. . . . (*A*, 361)

Underlying the many experiences of dialogue with his patients, what Williams hears is the poem of people's lives. "We begin to see that the underlying meaning of all they want to tell us and have always failed to communicate is the poem, the poem which their lives are being lived to realize. . . . And it is the actual words, as we hear them spoken under all circumstances, which contain it" (*A*, 361, 362). This underlying poem, or rhythm of people's lives trying to communicate itself, Williams sees as the gist or "rare presence," the inspiration for his poetry. "We must recover underlying meaning as realistically as we recover metal out of ore."

The poets whom Williams admires, those who use popular speech, "a Homer, a Villon," are poets who, like the doctor, could capture the "rumor" of ordinary speech and hear its "minutest variations. . . ." Both the doctor and the poet must be listeners, interpreters, looking for the conformations of speech in which "life is hid" (*A*, 362).

Williams not only learned to listen more carefully through his work as a physician, he learned to exercise his genius for "Negative Capability," his capacity to forget himself and live in the mystery of his patients' dramas. "I lost myself in the very properties of their minds: for the moment at least I actually became *them*, whoever they should be, so that when I detached myself from them at the end of a half-hour of intense concentration over some illness which was affecting them, it was as though I were reawakening from a sleep. For the moment I myself did not exist, nothing of myself affected me" (*A*, 356). This exercise of the imagination, connected with real life, helped Williams create the speech of characters outside himself with compassion and objectivity. The poet forgets himself in his creation of his characters as Shakespeare must have done. The last words of the sick old woman in Williams' poem "To an old Jaundiced Woman" remain in the reader's mind as they must have stayed in Williams'.

> I can't die
> —moaned the old
> jaundiced woman
> rolling her
> saffron eyeballs
> I can't die
> I can't die (*CEP*, 268)

In "Asphodel" it is Williams who "can't die," not until he has made amends with Flossie. This time the poet speaks in his own persona; having spoken eloquently for others, Williams must now bring his skills to bear for himself. He talks with characteristic directness: "Give me time, / time" (*PB*, 154).

Williams' tone in "Asphodel" is at once resigned and rebellious—transcendence of contradictions hums through the intricate structure of the triadic line. He achieved this calm tone through a lifetime of looking straight at the life around him and within, just as he examined his patients, and through a lifetime of "speaking straight ahead." The poet must look at the particulars of the poem carefully, without sentimentality. "That is the poet's business. Not to talk in vague categories but to write particularly, as a physician works, upon a patient, upon the thing before him, in the particular to discover the universal" (*A*, 391). An artist, to be any good, "must know his materials" and "must possess that really glandular perception of their uniqueness," which makes each word irreplaceable in the poem (*SE*, 233). Williams admired the sagas for the clear air of observation he found there, the clear facing of death. No "soft second light of dreaming" (*SE*, 67) in *The Iliad*, or for the poet Williams, though in "Asphodel" a "soft second light" of love does not blur the edges of the poem.

All traces of harshness have been washed away from the opening passage of "Asphodel"; what we hear is Williams' caring, his reaching out to speak to Flossie. The tercets, arranged on the page to cascade and return to stability at the margin of each new stanza, give a rising and falling motion to the poem. This movement suggests waves, or a cradle, or bodies rocking gently together. The poem brings flowers and rings with tenderness. Yet the line "save that it's green and wooden" gives us a clue that the poem has some angular, creaky steps within its rounded design, its circular framework. The poet himself is somewhat "wooden" in his efforts, shaky due to his illnesses, but his verses dance. In his vulnerable state, how does the poet reach out to the woman whom he feels he has wronged, whom he has come to love most deeply only in old age? "Asphodel" may be a graceful "flower to the mind," but it is also a journey: steps the poet had to take to make himself understood, steps that Flossie and the reader have to take to follow the poet to the place where contradictions and conflicts become part of the music.

Love is the source of healing in *Journey to Love*, the motivation for "Asphodel," and the heart of the poem. The poem begins and ends with a gift for Flossie, with the song of "Asphodel" and the evocation of a wedding ceremony. Love encompasses and assimilates the other themes of the poem, keeping it from becoming polemical or overly discursive. "What power has love but forgiveness?" Love becomes the aesthetic of the poem; the poet's need to express tender feelings is matched by the song's grace.

The ease of passage into the poem, the gentleness of the first section, may reflect the fact that Williams began to work on "Asphodel" while he and Flossie were together on vacation. Still recovering from his first stroke, Bill took Flossie to New York for two weeks, where they stayed at the New Weston Hotel.[9] On Saturday, March 1, 1952, the poet began to make handwritten notes for "Asphodel" on a hotel menu. The triadic lines tell of Asphodel "wet with morning dew," of an image emerging, a beginning, and of the poet's memory as a source of strength (YALC). The first section of "Asphodel," complete in itself as a lyric, published as "Work in Progress" (*The Desert Music*, 1954), is a personal statement (though not a private one), for Flossie.

The first section sings of Williams' personal history, of experiences the couple has shared; little distinction is made between shared literary experiences and other kinds of experiences, for "books / entered our lives," the poet reminds his wife. The poem *is* a life, recalling the expanse the couple has surveyed with "joined hands" since their marriage in 1912, making an apology for what the poet could not share with Flossie until after the fact, though his bones have "cried . . . / in the act" of separateness from her, of betrayal (*PB*, 158, 161). In Book II the poem leaves Flossie, to concern itself with death and the cruelties of history; it returns to her at the end of Book III, and at the end of the Coda. This movement is a paradigm of Williams' relationship with Flossie—though he may have strayed from her because of involvements with other women

9. Mariani, *A New World Naked*, 645.

and because of his absorption with poetry, he always returned home.[10]

That Williams married Flossie on the rebound from rejection by her beautiful and artistically accomplished sister Charlotte, we know from Williams' novel *The Build-Up*, and from his biographies.[11] He waited only three days after Charlotte had accepted his brother Ed to ask Florence to marry him. Did he propose to Flossie on an impulse? Out of rebellion against his brother? Or with an instinct that to build a creative life he would need a woman who could put up with his idiosyncracies, one who would be strong and stable enough to ride out the rough times? The dialogue between husband and wife in Williams' play *A Dream of Love* is telling.

> Myra:
> Do you remember what you said?
> Doc:
> Do *you*?
> Myra:
> —when I asked you if you loved me?
> Doc:
> No. What did I say?
> Myra:
> You said, "Love you? Hell no. I want to marry you."
> Doc:
> I don't believe I said that.
> Myra:
> Then I asked you, "Why do you want to marry me?" And you said, "To love you, I suppose."[12]

Early on in the play Doc dies in the arms of a lover, and his wife must respond to this betrayal. Doc speaks of his confessions to Myra as "the thrill of a perpetual recovery from an illness"; the "cure" is somewhat more problematic from the

10. *Ibid.*, 661–62.
11. William Carlos Williams, *The Build-Up* (New York, 1952), 260–64; Reed Whittemore, *William Carlos Williams: Poet from Jersey* (Boston, 1975), 61–76; Mariani, *A New World Naked*, 76–79.
12. William Carlos Williams, *Many Loves and Other Plays* (New York, 1961), 121.

wife's point of view.[13] Though Myra is made to witness her husband's affair, she still accepts his ghost when he comes home. Love is seen as cruelty, compassion, and, above all, as an act of the will. Williams will speak of love this way again in "The Ivy Crown," one of the poems that prefaces "Asphodel" (*PB*, 126).

In "Asphodel" Williams explains himself to Flossie.

> It was the love of love,
> the love that swallows up all else,
> a grateful love,
> a love of nature, of people,
> animals,
> a love engendering
> gentleness and goodness
> that moved me
> and *that* I saw in you. (*PB*, 160)

On a taped reading of this poem held in the Rutherford Public Library, Williams emphasized the word "you": Flossie *was* special.[14] Yet this gentleness and goodness, like the lily-of-the-valley, could be cloying, producing a recoil.

> I should have known
> though I did not,
> that the lily-of-the-valley
> is a flower makes many ill
> who whiff it. (*PB*, 160)

The story of a difficult marriage is embedded in "Asphodel." The poet alludes to his wanderings.

> Imagine you saw
> a field made up of women
> all silver-white.
> What should you do
> but love them? (*PB*, 159–60)

---

13. *Ibid.*, 213.
14. William Carlos Williams, "Asphodel, That Greeny Flower, Book I," recorded in April, 1954, at the University of Puerto Rico. Tape at the Rutherford Free Public Library. See Emily Mitchell Wallace, *A Bibliography of William Car-*

This passage recalls Rilke's "Third Duino Elegy," where the narrator explains the poet's erotic nature to a perplexed young woman.

> Look
> we don't love like flowers   out of a
>   single season   Where we love
> immemorial sap
>   mounts in our arms   O girl
>   this:
>   that we've loved in
>   us   not one, still to come, but all
> innumerable fermentation . . . .

A poetic sensibility, it seems (to Rilke and to Williams), presses the writer to love outside or beyond the bounds of domesticity.[15]

Flossie is no "Mädchen," and the references to Williams' inattentions, to his infidelities, are made gently, tastefully, "in figures," like Flossie's "dresses." The poet is direct, but his account is not as blunt as the fictional unfolding in *A Dream of Love.*

Williams is separate from Flossie in his early poems, in *Kora*, where she is off cleaning house as he meditates on art; in *Paterson*, where divorce is a leitmotif, where "Beautiful Thing" is a rape victim (*P*, 151–54). But in "Asphodel" the poet speaks to Flossie without disguise, for he needs her and is determined to reach her. Such honest speaking does not occur easily.

"I am extremely sexual in my desires: I carry them everywhere and at all times," Williams states on the first page of the "Foreword" to *The Autobiography.* His lyric poems are filled with allusions to erotic encounters, real or imagined. Nature is charged with the poet's erotic energy—even the fences become involved in the general excitement:

---

los Williams (Middletown, Conn., 1968), F14, p. 263, for a full description of contents.

15. "Rilke's Third Elegy Transposed," trans. George Quasha, *Caterpillar*, III/IV (1968), 207–208.

> the big tree smiles and glances
> upward.
> Tense with suppressed excitement
> the fences watch where the ground
> has humped an aching shoulder for
> the ecstasy. (*CEP*, 141)

Sex and the poem are interconnected throughout Williams' work. The poet has it in his power to restore nature through art, to put the "pink petal" "on / its stem / again"; Williams' erotic imagination is at work even in his old age (*PB*, 17).

While this erotic energy suffuses Williams' poetry, for the most part to the reader's delight, one wonders how Flossie felt about it all.[16] What was her place in this charged "field"? In his early poems Williams joked about his marriage, protesting with humor against public opinion. "I married you because I liked your nose. / I wanted you! . . . / in spite of all they'd say—" (*CEP*, 183). In *Journey to Love* we are told "a simple story. / Love is in season." Late in Williams' life he no longer jokes about love. Love becomes survival. "I love you / or I do not live / at all" (*PB*, 97, 124).

"Marriage has to be seen as a poem, as a thing," Williams writes.[17] Like the poem it has to be worked on to reach its clearest version. In the late poems, as Williams pursued his search for a "redeeming language," he also created a poetry of affirmation of his abiding love for Flossie.

As an old man, Williams learned to love Flossie with a new tenderness and consideration. It was Flossie who took care of him during his late illnesses, and she who kept him company when he could no longer stray. Spending so much time with Flossie, under her protection, must have caused Williams to reflect on his debt to her. In an interview in 1958, Williams confided in Gail Turnbull, "Oh Floss, what she's put up with.

16. On a typed worksheet for Book III, numbered p. 10, Williams writes of Flossie, "Yet you do not forgive / many another." YALC.

17. "The poem . . . is called also a marriage. All these terms have to be redefined, a marriage has to be seen as a thing. The poem is made of things— on a field." *A*, 333.

I don't know how. I was pretty raw in those days. Some of the
women, too. It was all wrong . . . I wonder what she thinks of
me" (*Int*, 93). In the late poems, the renewed love of the poet
for his wife becomes a constant theme. In "To Be Recited to
Flossie on Her Birthday," the poet affirms his love while acknowledging the complexities of experience he and Flossie
have been through.

> Let him who may
> among the continuing lines
> seek out
> that tortured constancy
> affirms
> where I persist
> let me say
> across cross purposes
> that the flower bloomed
> struggling to assert itself
> simply under
> the conflicting lights. . . . (*PB*, 35)

Williams' expression of love in the late poems is earned, not
easy or sentimental; he and his wife had journeyed together
over difficult terrain.

In *Journey to Love* the poet remembers how hard it was to get
to the place where his "heart" (as opposed to his body?) "is
innocent" (*PB*, 82). Like music, love transcends the sorry
facts now. In "The Ivy Crown" Williams describes the way his
love has changed through the imagination, surmounted conflicts as he and Flossie have grown old together.

> At our age the imagination
>   across the sorry facts
>   lifts us
> to make roses
>   stand before thorns.
>   Sure
> love is cruel
>   and selfish
>   and totally obtuse—

```
            at least, blinded by the light,
                     young love is.
                               But we are older,
        I to love
                     and you to be loved
                               we have,
            no matter how,
                     by our wills survived
                               to keep
            the jeweled prize
                     always
                               at our finger tips.
        We will it so
                     and so it is
                               past all accident. (PB, 126)
```

Love, like poetry, is seen as an act of creative will.

In "Asphodel" the theme of forgiveness rises above other concerns. "What power has love but forgiveness?" The opening music of Book III is the poem's refrain; though the line occurs only once in the poem, it sounds the poem's deepest source and recurs in the reader's mind (*PB*, 169). Williams is asking Flossie's forgiveness for the hurt he has caused her— though he tells us that he does not come "with confessions of my faults, / I have confessed, / all of them" (*PB*, 170). The poem is a confession that has done with confession—Williams' love of contradictions shines through even here. Williams comes "proudly / as to an equal / to be forgiven," for the poem is rich with his own love and forgiveness (*PB*, 170, 171). Why should the poet have to forgive Flossie? Perhaps that "love that swallowed up all else," that "grateful love" he felt for her, also caused him some anger. Perhaps Flossie could have had more of "Helen in her heart." The tone of "Asphodel" sings of the poet's forgiveness,[18] of release from self torture; forgiveness of

18. On a typed worksheet, n.p., YALC, Williams says to Flossie, with reference to "all women / who have offended (her)": "It is an artist's failing / to seek and to yield such forgiveness. / It will cure us both." He adds, "Let us / keep it to ourselves." The published version reads: "Let us / keep it to ourselves but trust it," placing emphasis on trust rather than secrecy. Another

the "niggardly" minds, the critics who ignored him, forgiveness of those involved in the "witch hunts." Measure is the key to the poem's success; the poem metes out an extra measure of mercy and love with "justice," its truth of form.

---

typed worksheet, part of a section marked "The River of Heaven," in handscript, p. 7, reads: "It is to be loved by you and to be sure of it / faulty as you are / as the whole human race is faulty." Williams rinsed the final poem of these pronouncements.

CHAPTER TWO

To Find a Technique of Verse

Williams "fought and fought and fought a lifetime" until he "hit the fusion of language and meter" in "Asphodel," where formal sureness expresses love with bright ceremony (*Int*, 48). He viewed the achievement of the triadic line, the measure of "Asphodel," as one of his major accomplishments, though he continued to work at stylistic change in later poems for *Pictures from Brueghel*. He had to overcome obstacles in his work toward the form of the late poems, as he had to cross "desert places" in his life in order to survive. Working against the tradition of British prosody challenged Williams to listen for the new, for the American idiom. Lack of formal certainty must have been frustrating at times, but "formless interims" did not deter Williams; some poets thrive by pushing the rudder and haulers away. Critical ignorance about Williams' efforts spurred him to work harder to try to articulate his poetic theories; yet critical indifference and ignorance also hurt the poet and the person, and cannot be rationalized as a good. Critical misunderstanding slowed down Williams' acceptance as a major American poet. His poems, theories, and his life worked together with an articulateness that stuttered at first, becoming a sure and graceful syncopation in his later years.

In the "Preface" to his *Selected Essays* Williams writes, ". . . it is principally about the poem that I have written critically in

my life. All the emotion that is involved in the making and defining of the poem is brought out" (n.p.). In his essays,
letters, articles, and speeches, Williams wrote consistently
and with passionate interest about making and defining the
poem. He was not, as the critics thought of him until late in
his life, "a rough sort of blindman" in his writing of poetry
(*SL*, 299). On the contrary, Williams took pride in the fabric of
his theories about poetry just as he did in his craft. The theories nourished the poems, kept Williams alert to the technical
innovations he sought for verse.

Williams' close attention to the details of poetic technique
enables us to see clearly what the poet thought of his own material, how he viewed his development and his place in modern poetry. His theories on the "American idiom" and the importance of the "local," his observations on the need for a new
"measure" or musical pace in modern poetry, are repeated
hundreds of times throughout his writings on poetics. Re-
stating his theories gave Williams an opportunity to develop
his thoughts fully. For example, though Williams stresses the
importance of the "local" in his 1920–1921 statements for the
magazine *Contact*, he states his goals briefly: "We *Contact*, aim
to emphasize the local phase of the game of writing" (*SE*, 29).
The vigor of Williams' critical statements in the 1920s has its
own aesthetic value, corresponding to the "compression,
colour, speed, and accuracy" that Marianne Moore admired
in his experimental poetry of this period.[1] But fullness of expression may be sacrificed to speed and emphasis in the early
critical statements; besides, Williams as a young poet was
"blazing a path" that he could not as yet see the turns of.
In the late writings on theory we find complete statements
on poetics, in which Williams is able to elaborate on all of
his ideas. The section called "The American Idiom" in the
1958–1959 essay "Measure" contains seven pages of clear, un-
hurried prose. The late essay not only defines "The American

1. Marianne Moore, "Kora in Hell, by William Carlos Williams," *Contact*,
Summer, 1921, pp. 5–8. Quoted by Paul Mariani in *William Carlos Williams:
The Poet and His Critics* (Chicago, 1975), 14.

Idiom" but goes on to consider the moral implications of its use.[2] The completeness and fullness of statement and feeling that we find in the late poems match Williams' critical understanding. He was working "to his theory."

The repetition of theory throughout Williams' work enables us to see how the poet worked, and with what faith. Williams could live with mystery and contradictions in his search for new forms, but he needed to affirm his creative powers, to assert his faith by means of his theories. Speaking of his youth, Williams says, "The thing I cannot quite name was there then. My writing, the necessity for a continued assertion, the need for me to go on will not let me stop" (*A*, 288). In his theories, Williams challenged himself to tasks: the more he predicted an innovation, the more likely he was to effect it.

In his essays and letters Williams documents each stage of his poetic development or education. He states his goals and celebrates his successes. He was an innovator in the use of natural diction, incorporating conversational rhythms of speech into the poem, cleansing the poem of "poetic" vocabulary and inversions of phrase. But Williams saw that his main task was to break down the traditional iambic pentameter line in favor of a flexible but ordered line, sensitive to the rhythms of contemporary speech. This was to be the work of a lifetime.

Though Keats and Shakespeare were Williams' earliest poetic influences, Walt Whitman played a more significant role in his development as an original American poet. Whitman, the first American poet who interested Williams, had dreamed of a common language with America as its source. Whitman had shown the need for a distinctly American form of verse to express the American experience. But Williams insists that Whitman did not go far enough, that Whitman did not have enough control over his art to add to our knowledge of technique once he had broken the traditional line. Of Whitman's place in the history of poetry, Williams says, "His misfortune

2. "Measure: —a loosely assembled essay on poetic measure" (in folder ZA 154 of the YALC). Undated, the essay includes letters and notes from 1958.

is that he came in on the destructive phase. And while he broke down staid usages, he found nothing to take their place, merely scattered himself broadcast."[3]

Williams frequently refers to Whitman with a mixed tone of admiration and disdain. For if Whitman is a hero whose work represents a breakthrough in American poetry, he is also the progenitor and "rival" (*SE*, "Preface," n.p.); Williams must wrestle Whitman to the ground before he can truly accept him as a source, then transform him into a friend and contemporary. Williams continually strengthens his ideas by writing against the apparent disorderliness of Whitman's style.

To Whitman's credit, "Free verse was his great idea" (ELG, 23). But "free verse was chaos" to Williams' mind.[4] The break with tradition was Whitman's first and only formal accomplishment. "Whitman was right in breaking our bounds but, having no valid restraints to hold him, went wild. He didn't know any better" (*SE*, 339). Whitman "slipped off"[5] as a poet because he was "preoccupied with the great ideas of the time . . . but after all, poems are made out of words, not ideas" (ELG, 23). In his letters Williams depicts Whitman, not himself, as the "instinctive blindman" who destroyed classic measure almost by chance. "Witlessly, but taking his cue out of the air, Whitman was in his so-called free verse only initiating a new measure" (*SL*, 332). At times Williams sets Whitman up as his foil; Whitman plays Dr. Watson to Williams' Sherlock. For it is Williams who intends to be the conscious artist, to go beyond the "necessary phase"[6] of free verse and find the line that will provide us with the "solution of the problem of modern verse" (*SL*, 334).

3. William Carlos Williams, "Introduction" to *Transfigured Night: Poems by Byron Vazakas* (New York, 1946), x.

4. ELG, 23; William Carlos Williams, "Letter on Pound," *Quarterly Review of Literature*, V (1950), 301.

5. "On Whitman" (C153, UB). Catalogue numbers are found in Neil Baldwin and Steven Meyers, *The Manuscripts and Letters of William Carlos Williams in the Poetry Collection: Lockwood Memorial Library, State University of New York at Buffalo: A Descriptive Catalogue* (Boston, 1978).

6. Williams, "Letter on Pound," 301.

Whitman becomes a touchstone by which Williams measures his own and other poets' progress toward establishing
the new metrics. Writing of Byron Vazakas' *Transfigured Night:
Poems* in 1946, Williams applauds a sense of order that is missing in Whitman's verse. "He [Vazakas] has done away with the
poetic line as we know it, a clean sweep, not a vestige of
it left. This is far beyond Whitman's looseness. . . . He has
found a *measure* based not upon convention, but upon music
for his reliance. . . ."[7] Though Williams had placed Pound as
well as Whitman at the beginning of modern American verse,
Williams insisted that there was an important difference: ". . .
Pound was *disciplined*," a quality of mind required of the modern poet (*Int*, 43).

Williams invokes Whitman over and over again in his writings on poetics, in connection with the contemporary poet's
will to continue the invention of American verse. This repetition of a name is also an invocation and incantation—Whitman
represents a source of American poetry, and Williams wills
himself to be a source as well. The repetition of Whitman's
name throughout Williams' writings also alerts us to the
unity of Williams' theories, a unity based not only on bulk
and repetition but on implied connections and equations
gradually built up. Whitman's name occurs frequently in the
late writings in connection with mention of Einstein and with
Williams' assertion of the need for a new poetic measure in a
relativistic age. Whitman comes to represent not only America and the common language, iconoclasm and formlessness,
but the poetic line itself. This line begins with Whitman's free
fall and leads to what Charles Olson calls "Projective Verse,"
to fresh footing in poetic space.

Williams was proud of his iconoclasm, but also of his mission to restore and repair. He saw the work of restructuring
modern verse as the central work of modern poetry. "I continue to refer to the construction, the reconstitution of the
poem as my major theme . . . the present-day necessity" (*A*,
333). Williams considered his extensive writing on poetics as

7. Williams, "Introduction" to *Transfigured Night*, xiv.

part of the constructive phase, a laying of groundwork for the new poetics.

The poet's tendency to celebrate theory and technique, particularly his own theory and technique, has been depicted as old-fashioned American salesmanship. Reed Whittemore views Williams' excitement over the new measure and the triadic line in this way:

[Williams] insisted over and over again that what he had himself at last arrived at prosodically, his "variable foot," would probably prove to be his most important contribution to the art. Sometimes when he was feeling grand and messianic he sounded as if the world revolution was beginning with the variable foot, and in this expectation also he was displaying not a Marxist line but the line of an old-fashioned American entrepreneur, one setting forth into the future with his own better mousetrap.[8]

But Williams' talk about poetics is more important than mere sales talk. The critical writing helps the poet to focus his attention on problems of craft, to attain a conscious mastery of the art. The achievement of an American poetry, written with such discipline and consciousness of craft, would add dignity to the new American poetry.

In his talks and writings on poetics, Williams tries to dispel America's negative self-image as to its cultural importance. "If America or American is a stigma upon us, it is because we have not yet been able to raise the place we inhabit to such an imaginative level that it shall have currency in the world of the mind."[9] Such a lifting of place of mind is a tremendous imaginative task; at times Williams' talk about the new poetics becomes charged with his sense of his difficult mission. The poet *is* trying to sell America to itself, to convince a resistant or uninterested audience to come into closer relationship to the life around it through modern American poetry.

As Ted Whittaker puts it, the poet's way of looking at the world becomes a common good at least in part through his

8. Reed Whittemore, *William Carlos Williams: Poet from Jersey* (Boston, 1975), 315–16.
9. "Memory Script of a talk delivered at Briarcliff Junior College November 29, 1945: VERSE AS EVIDENCE OF THOUGHT," 7 (C92, UB).

ability to promote a unifying myth. "The job of a poet is to create a myth, a way of looking at the world and the life in it. Add to his skill and insight that of a good adman (unless the poet himself be the adman of the power élite) and his views become the mental currency of the commons. We lack a unifying myth today. . . ."[10]

Williams' insistence on the need for new forms in poetry, his promotion of his technical achievements discovered in his mature years, comes through to the reader with a sense of urgency and conviction. Williams speaks with the excitement of a man who has had a vision he cannot fully define, or one who is on the edge of a vision watching himself grope for shape. As he described his talk on poetics in 1945, "This is a sentience, a feeling, a groping . . . for a new metrical pattern in the speech."[11] If Williams' will to share his quest for new forms comes to us at times like a sales pitch, perhaps this is because the salesman is a prevalent American persona. We speak according to the rhythms of our environment, Williams teaches us.

Williams was aware that his fervor for formal innovations might come across as messianic or as a sales pitch. In his talk "Verse as Evidence of Thought" at Briarcliff Junior College (1945) he reassured his audience: "Take it easy. I have nothing to sell. I'm not a religionist in any sense. I'm speaking for the poem." To explain his sense of the importance of his work at his craft, Williams stated, "For what else is there for us in our lives but to communicate with each other as completely as we are able, and in ways which give us all our deepest and most comprehensive agreements. If you are interested in that, then you are interested in poetry. It is nothing for sale."[12] For Williams the development of form has a human purpose. In the poems of *Journey to Love*, including "Asphodel," the poet communicates with Flossie and with us "as completely as he is able."

10. Ted Whittaker, "Presumptions," *Open Letter*, III (April, 1966), 22.
11. "A New Line is a New Measure," 15 (C41, UB).
12. "Briarcliff Junior College Talk," 4.

Even Williams' talk to himself has an urging on to it: "I *am* a poet! I am . . ." (*PB*, 120). In his struggle against the Establishment and traditional prosody Williams had to give himself the encouragement he needed. As a poet working in a new vein he explicated his poetics as carefully as he could for his readers. Certainly the critics would not do this work for him until he was well in his sixties.

The push in Williams' voice also tells us that he was competing with some "'strong men' of letters" (*SL*, 312). For most of his life at writing Williams competed for attention with Eliot and with Pound, though for thirty years Williams came up short. Eliot in particular was a spur, for he represented to Williams a betrayal of the life of American poetics to the traditional forms of British prosody. The attention given to Eliot's *The Waste Land* hit Williams hard, as he tells us in the *Autobiography*: "It [*The Waste Land*] wiped out our world as if an atom bomb had been dropped upon it and our brave sallies into the unknown were turned to dust" (174). America was at war with England in Williams' argument with Eliot (Did England even know about the battle?) but there was more to it than that, as Williams admitted in a later interview. "He [Eliot] was giving up America. And maybe my attachment to my father, who was English and who had never become an American citizen influenced me because I was—You know, the Oedipus complex, between father and son—I resented him being English and not being American. And that was when Eliot was living in England and had given up America" (*Int*, 47).

In a letter to Robert Lowell, Williams speaks with characteristic directness about the nature of his ambition. "I must make the new meter out of whole cloth, I've got to know the necessity back of it. I am not driven by the search for personal distinction, I don't want to appear in person. But I want to see the unknown shine, like a sunrise. I want to see that overpowering mastery that will inundate the whole scene penetrate to that last jungle" (*SL*, 313).

Williams sought to be a master at the craft of poetry. In an interview in 1951, he spoke of theory as part of an artist's work, necessary to mastery: ". . . the better artist he is, the better he's able to recognize what is good and *why* it's good. . . . He must have his theories, as Pasteur said, he must work to them, and so he becomes what has been termed in the past a master—a man who knows what everything means, knows why he put it down, can take it apart and put it together again and still have it as spontaneous as ever. In fact, Yeats said you must labor to be beautiful" (*Int*, 85). A continued interest in theory sharpens the poet's faculties, improving his artistry. According to Williams, old age becomes an advantage to the conscious artist.

I think the young man is likely to be carried away by his passion; but the old man, if he is wise, knows *why* he is writing a good poem. I like to think of the Japanese print maker Hokusai who said that (he lived to be ninety-nine) when he arrived at age a hundred, every dot on his paper would be significant. If your interest is in theory, as Pasteur's interest was in theory, and your mind is alive and you're trying to improve your poems technically, you will produce the work, and will never cease to produce it. In fact, I hope that with my last breath I shall make an addition to my technical equipment so that I will feel a little more satisfied to think of myself than I have been in the past. I think the older you get, provided you don't abuse your faculties, the better you're likely to be as an artist. (*Int*, 61, 62)

What may appear simple, prints by the Japanese master, paintings of Paul Klee, or lines from *Paterson V*, are not simple matters to achieve:

>   you cannot be
>   an artist
>   by mere ineptitude
>   The dream
>   is in pursuit!
>   The neat figures of
>   Paul Klee
>   fill the canvas
>   but that
>   is not the work
>   of a child . (*P*, 258–59)

There is nothing childlike about Williams' technique of verse. In these lines from *Paterson V*, where Williams calls the reader's attention to a sophisticated kind of simplicity, the poet is using a shortened version of the three-ply or triadic line, which took him forty years to develop. The triumph is not a theory of poetics, but the poem itself; theory is embedded unobtrusively in the poem. The poem always comes first for Williams: "We must never make the mistake of trying to substitute the materials of a new territory for the great and universal power of the art itself" (*SE*, 272).

The poem must be earned; initiation is difficult. As Williams wrote to Denise Levertov, "Writing, good writing . . . is never easy." Williams advises her that "practice, practice, practice is what makes the artist. . . ." A key to good writing, Williams insists, is to learn to pare and cut, as he tells Levertov: "Cut and cut again whatever you write—while you leave by your art no trace of your cutting—and the final utterance will remain packed with what you have to say. The stream does not ripple or at best go wild save by the swiftness of its flow, as well as by the obstruction it encounters." Then Williams emphasizes a point that seems to go beyond technique: "But in the end you must say whatever you have to say, without honesty completely outspoken you will not succeed in moving yourself or the world." [13]

The richness of the content of the poem, and the rhythmic character of its flow, will be the result of obstructions artfully overcome. In his essay on Kay Boyle's stories, Williams writes that some effects of the struggle with the materials should show up in the style.

The quality of Kay Boyle's stories has in it all of this strain. They are simple, quite simple, but an aberrant American effect is there in the style. There is something to say and one says it. That's writing. But to say it one must have it alive with the overtones which give not a type of statement but an actual statement that is alive, marked with a gait and appearance which show it to be the motion of an individual who has suffered it and brought it into fact. This is style. Excellence comes from overcoming difficulties. (*I*, 342)

13. William Carlos Williams, "Letters to Denise Levertov," *Stony Brook*, I/II (Post-Fall, 1968), 163, 164.

In this statement Williams equates the struggle for earned simplicity and for directness with both the American idiom and with style itself. Surely "Asphodel" embodies this style, this phase of Williams' American idiom, as the poem moves with the "gait" of one "who has suffered it and brought it into fact."

Underlying all of Williams' theories there is a poet who loves contradictions, who embraces them with glee. Negative Capability allows the poet to take on many voices, even in his own theories, without worrying over the contradictions, and permits him to dramatize his understanding that a truth may contain its opposite. "After thirty years staring at one true phrase he discovered its opposite was true also," Williams writes of himself in *Kora* (57). The theorist in Williams stabilized his work at poetry, enabling him to experiment with his lines while meditating on problems of technique. The poet in Williams was then free to embrace process and movement. "When eyes are humming birds who'll tie them with a lead string?" (*K*, 11, 12).

With his love of contradictions, Williams never veered from the conviction that poetry is work, not Freudian compensation, not fanciful dreaming, but hard work. "The better work men do is always done under stress and at great personal cost" (*I*, 101). Struggle is not undertaken for its own sake, but results from a commitment to work. Williams is not Rimbaud— he does not suggest that the poet break himself down for the sake of the poem, but that the poem's limits be broken for the poet's sake. "But good God, it is the breaking of the barriers to our lives that is human, not the dashing of ourselves to pieces on granite that we should praise" (*I*, 341).

Williams understood that the modern poet's work is part of a long tradition of poetry, that even the breaking down of the traditional depends on a knowledge of tradition. The struggle for simplicity, for the pared line that reflects the American idiom, can come about only through an understanding of what has been written before. Williams complains in an essay that college students do not understand how many centuries of work it takes to prepare for an artistic creation.

They cannot know that for even a Mozart ages of work have to be done by generations of sweating predecessors, poets (laborers), before the simplest expressions can come to flower.

Even Bobby Burns reaped the work done in the Middle English Period—from the thirteenth century and earlier—broke up the old fourteener, giving him his ballad form. It is wise to remember the long progress of English, as its poems demonstrate, from the Anglo-Saxon rigidities—by *invention* through many changes of form.

According to Williams, the conventional poetic forms based on English rules of prosody will have to be broken down. "*Everything* has to be broken down, not cynically, not without a deep sense of its old dignity, to get at the essential; the *formal* unit in its purity. . . ."[14]

Always, the creation of the new forms in poetry will require work. "And do not believe, I keep repeating, that the form of the age will spontaneously appear. . . . Nothing could be more fatuous. It is the work, the exhausting work of the artist who (not as a vain type) but by working in the guild, the traditions of his art, as an inheritor of all the skills of the past will MAKE the world today." The end of the poet's labor is to invent a new structure that reflects the rhythm and truth of his time. "But to invent we have actually, as the word radical itself intimates, to return to the root. Return to the simpler constructive elements of the line."[15]

Despite Williams' respect for poetic traditions and his constant meditation in his works on the nature of poetry and on the serious responsibility of the poet, despite his prolific output of poetry and fiction, even the best of poets still referred to Williams' work as "anti-poetic." Wallace Stevens used this term in his *Preface* to the 1934 edition of Williams' *Collected Poems*. Part of the problem derived from Stevens' misunder-

---

14. William Carlos Williams, "An Approach to the Poem," in *English Institute Essays* (New York, 1947), 56, 57.
15. *Ibid.*, 61.

standing of Williams' use of prose passages within poems. Williams thought enough of himself as a poet in a tradition of poets to react strongly: he writes to Parker Tyler that prose, which adds a "metrical continuity between all word use" is "*not* an anti-poetic device, the repeating of which piece of miscalculation makes me want to puke" (*SL*, 263).

Williams reacted strongly not because of egotism, but because of the seriousness of the misunderstanding. Not only Williams' use of prose, but ironically his use of natural rhythms of speech in poetry and his treatment of common themes and everyday experiences, led to Stevens' confusion. It is a deep respect for the ordinary as a potential source for poetry that makes Williams respond with such fury to the term "anti-poetic." In the poem "To All Gentleness," Williams includes lines to this effect: "And they speak, / euphemistically, of the anti-poetic! / Garbage. Half the world ignored . . ." (*CLP*, 24).

The interest of poetry resides in the imagination's treatment of things. "The fact is that in a work of art there is no difference between the beautiful and the ugly. It is all the same material for the work of the imagination."[16] Williams' poetry is enriched by its substance, by the fact that he has something to say. Yet his trust is in the imagination and in the poet's skill at arranging, in style and the ability of a flexible line to communicate with the world.

In a letter dated January 5, 1950, to R. L. Beum (a critic who saw that neither Williams' materials nor his treatment of them was in any way "anti-poetic"), Williams writes as if he must still fight against the misconception about his work propagated by Stevens in 1934. In his letter to Beum, Williams makes a strikingly clear statement of his views.

Wallace Stevens (in an introduction to one of my books of poems) invented the fallacy of my use of "anti-poetic" materials to enhance the poetic materials in my poems. And every ass with nothing to say has copied his dictum. I have protested against this falsity of Stevens' first observation whenever it was possible to do so.

16. "Briarcliff Junior College Talk," 9.

Rodman [a reviewer], has fallen into the old groove. Certainly you are right and he is wrong when he says that I have "applied the method of arranging *anti-poetic* material in prose cadences" for any reason whatever. I have never used prose as prose in a poem. I have always insisted that standard english verse is stone cold, dead, finished. I have wanted something else. The syntactical cadences *discoverable in prose* but used as metric are the true sources of my verse. Why are we so stupid that we cannot see something so elementary?[17]

The reader hears the "syntactical cadences discoverable in prose" in the late poems: "Hear me out. / Do not turn away."

Williams' disciplined directness and simplicity of style was new to modern poetry. He focuses in his poetry on the things and people he sees around him, as we discover in the details of a poem like "Proletarian Portrait."

> A big young bareheaded woman
> in an apron
>
> Her hair slicked back standing
> on the street
>
> One stockinged foot toeing
> the sidewalk
>
> Her shoe in her hand. Looking
> intently into it
>
> She pulls out the paper insole
> to find the nail
>
> That has been hurting her   (*CEP*, 101)

Williams writes without flourish; his pared lines reveal his craftsmanship. The poet seeks to focus his attention on the materials at hand, to keep his style sharp and unsentimental. Williams' explanation to John Thirlwall of his attitude toward poetry, of his aim as a poet, is a key statement for understanding the poet's work.

I've always wanted to fit poetry into the life around us . . . because I love poetry. I'm not the type of poet who looks only at the rare thing. I want to use the words we speak and to describe the things we see, as far as it can be done. I abandoned the rare world of H. D. and Ezra Pound. Poetry should be brought into the world where we live and

---

17. William Carlos Williams to R. Beum, January 5, 1950 (uncatalogued, UB).

not be so recondite, so removed from the people. To bring poetry out of the clouds and down to earth I still believe possible. Using common words in a rare manner will advance the cause of the Poem infinitely.[18]

Williams saw the business of the poet as communication. In the poem "January Morning," Williams addresses his English grandmother and explains some of his motives for writing poetry.

> All this—
> was for you, old woman.
> I wanted to write a poem
> that you would understand.
> For what good is it to me
> if you can't understand it?
> But you got to try hard—   (*CEP*, 165–66)

The straightforward syntax of this verse and the simple vocabulary demonstrate what the poet is saying.

The fact that Williams' poem "To a Poor Old Woman" is so well known does not detract from its richness as a poem; in fact, the popularity of the poem is a tribute to Williams' desire to write well of ordinary events.

> To a Poor Old Woman
>
> munching a plum on
> the street a paper bag
> of them in her hand
>
> They taste good to her
> They taste good
> to her. They taste
> good to her
>
> You can see it by
> the way she gives herself
> to the one half
> sucked out in her hand
>
> Comforted
> a solace of ripe plums

18. John C. Thirlwall, "William Carlos Williams' 'Paterson': The Search for the Redeeming Language—A Personal Epic in Five Parts," in James Laughlin (ed.), *New Directions in Prose and Poetry: 17* (Norfolk, Conn., 1961), 8.

> seeming to fill the air
> They taste good to her   (*CEP*, 99)

The line breaks give a syncopation to the poem; sentences broken in midstream—"They taste good / to her"—lead the reader expectantly on to the next line. Repetition emphasizes enjoyment, while the variation in the line breaks calls attention to the materials of the poem, to word-play and rhythmic possibilities.

Williams taught Americans that their experiences are important and should be considered as important as any experience of European culture. "We can't believe that we poor colonials . . . we poor people who are not living in the great centers of Europe could have anything happen in our lives important enough to be put down in words and given a *form*. But everything in our lives, if it's sufficiently authentic to our lives and touches us deeply enough with a certain amount of feeling, is capable of being organized into a form which can be a poem" (*Int*, 17). It is the imaginative treatment of our own experience which counts.

In order to make our experiences tangible and direct, Williams sought to avoid symbolism in his poetry; he wanted to keep the poem rich without adding the usual poetic devices. In a letter to Kenneth Burke, Williams refers to "a desire on both our parts to find some basis for avoiding the tyranny of the symbolic without sacrificing fullness of imagery." The avoidance of symbols, for Williams, has to do with cutting down the distance between the reader and the sensual reality of the word and experience. "My whole intent, in my life," he says to Burke, "has been, as with you, to find a basis (in poetry, in my case) for the actual" (*SL*, 257). In the 1931 essay "Against the Weather: A Study of the Artist," Williams asserts more vigorously that "no symbolism is acceptable. No symbolism can be permitted to obscure the real purpose, to lift the world of the senses to the level of the imagination and so give it new currency" (*SE*, 213).

Williams saw a shift from ideas in poetry to words themselves as characteristic of modernism: he considers Pound's

Cantos as indicative of "the principal move in imaginative writing today—that away from the word as symbol toward the word as reality" (*SE*, 107). Speaking of Cézanne's impact on modernism, Williams continues to consider this theme: "It is the taking of that step over from feeling to the imaginative object, on the cloth, on the page, that defined the term, the modern term—a work of art. . . . It is to *play*. . . . The key, the master-key to the age was that jump from the feeling to the word itself" (*A*, 380–81).

In Williams' poetry words appear to present themselves as facts of the poet's existence, implying his acceptance of words and of the natural world.[19] While Williams' work may not be wholly free of the tensions between the "abysses of subjectivity" and the external world, the reader feels more at ease in the flow of natural diction than he or she might feel in crossing the threshold into a more traditionally constructed poem, or world of artifice. In the late poems Williams resolves the tension between the inner world of memory and the external world of newspaper accounts by juxtaposition and syncopation. The tension between worlds creates a definite resolution: "Only the imagination is real!" (*PB*, 179). Even this statement charged with questions for the reader about the nature of the mind, of poetry, about the sources of language and its powers, is made simply, directly.

Robert Lowell's understanding of the directness and hard-won simplicity of Williams' poetry can be seen in the effects that it had on his own style. He felt the impact of Williams' treatment of the word itself as reality in his apparently simple diction, his use of natural rhythms of speech in poetry. Lowell's description of the change in his style after reading Williams helps us to see the astringent, purifying force and the revitalizing powers of Williams' verse. This description represents the impact of the American idiom on the British tradition in American poetry. Lowell recalls his early work at verse:

19. See J. Hillis Miller's discussion of Williams' sensibility in *Poets of Reality: Six Twentieth Century Writers* (Cambridge, Mass., 1966), esp. 292, 288.

When I arrived at college . . . I began to rummage through the Cambridge bookshops. I found books that must have been looking for a buyer since the students days of Trumbull Stickney: soiled metrical treatises written by obscure English professors in the eighteen-nineties. They were full of glorious things: rising rhythm, falling rhythm, feet with Greek names, stanzas from Longfellow's *Psalm of Life,* John Drinkwater and Swinburne. Nothing seemed simpler than meter. I began experiments with an exotic foot, short, long, two shorts, then fell back on iambics. My material now took twice as many words, and I rolled out Spenserian stanzas on Job and Jonah surrounded by recently seen Nantucket scenery. Everything I did . . . had a timeless, hackneyed quality. All this was ended by reading Williams. It was as though some homemade ship, part Spanish galleon, part paddlewheels, kitchen pots and elastic bands and worked by hand, had anchored to a filling station.

He pays Williams the tribute of calling him "a model and a liberator. . . . His style is almost a common style and even what he claims for it—*the American Style.*"[20]

Yet in emphasizing Williams' common style, Lowell does not wish to make this style sound easy.

I have emphasized Williams' simplicity and nakedness and have no doubt been misleading. His idiom comes from many sources, from speech and reading, both of various kinds; the blend, which is his own invention, is generous and even exotic. Few poets can come near to his wide clarity and dashing rightness with words, his dignity and almost Alexandrian modulations of voice. His short lines often speed up and simplify hugely drawn out and ornate sentence structures. I once typed out his direct but densely observed poem, "The Semblables," in a single prose paragraph. Not a word or its placing had been changed, but the poem had changed into a piece of smothering, magnificent rhetoric, much more like Faulkner than the original Williams.[21]

This appreciation intensifies our interest in looking at the work behind Williams' achievement of stylistic simplicity.

A consistent concern in Williams' writings, one that reinforces his attempt to find a poetics that is at home in its environment, is his concern for the "local." The concept of the

20. Robert Lowell, "William Carlos Williams," in J. Hillis Miller (ed.), *William Carlos Williams: A Collection of Critical Essays* (Englewood Cliffs, 1966), 156, 158.
21. *Ibid.,* 156–57.

local, achieved through the American idiom, is a unifying idea in Williams' poetic theory.

If we turn to Williams' essay, we find that Williams defined the local as "the sense of being attached with integrity to actual experience" (*SE*, 118). The local, then, is the poet's intimacy with the experience in and around him that gives authenticity to his or her work. As Williams put it, ". . . I have been watching speech in my own environment from which I continually expect to discover whatever of new is being reflected about the world. I have no interest, as far as observation goes, in the cosmic. . . . art can be made of anything—provided it be seen, smelt, touched, apprehended and understood to be what it is—the flesh of a constantly repeated permanence" (*SL*, 129–30). The local, the immediate, seen and depicted as a sensual reality, becomes universal. Williams argued with Pound that the local was not just "American": "I'm no more sentimental about 'murika' than Li Po was about China or Shakespeare about Yingland. . . . All I care about is to write" (*SL*, 139, 140). Williams did not wish to be misunderstood about this. "As to the use of the term American when attached to a work of art, I confess it is of no importance unless it is intended to signify that excellence has no particular locale." The local is interchangeable with the idea of place, with the love of tangible particulars and immediacy of experience transmitted through art. "Place, rightly understood, means any place, but it must be a place, some place, a particular place, and whatever place the abstractionist finds, he finds, if it has been touched by human hands, that it also has a name. It is this name only which is usable by the artist."[22] Memory, too, can be a tangible place, touched by the heart, as we see in the late poems.

The "American idiom" is one aspect of the poet's style, the way an American poet translates contact with this environment into language. Williams defines the "American idiom" as "the language we speak in the United States. It is character-

22. William Carlos Williams, "Axioms," in Bram Dijkstra (ed.), *A Recognizable Image: William Carlos Williams on Art and Artists* (New York, 1978), 175–76.

ized by certain differences from the language used by cultured Englishmen, being completely free from all influences which can be summed up as having to do with 'the Establishment.' This, pared to essentials, is the language which governed Walt Whitman in his choice of words. It constituted a revolution in language." Unfortunately, according to Williams, scholars have hidden our language from us behind "tradition." The American idiom "had been driven into a secondary place by our scholars, those rats that had abandoned it to seek salvage elsewhere in safer places. . . . 'The Establishment' fixed in its commitments, has arrived at its last stand, the iambic pentameter, blank verse, the verse of Shakespeare and Marlowe which give it its prestige. A full stop."[23] It is up to modern American poets to find a more suitable form for contemporary verse.

Williams identifies language "pared to essentials" with the American idiom. He speaks of the American style as one that is straightforward and sharp. In reference to Gertrude Stein's work he writes, "Unbound thinking has to be done with straight, sharp words. Call them nails to hold together the joints of the new architecture" (*SE*, 163–64). The words have an immediate quality: "You can't quite kill the love of the actual which underlies all American enjoyment" (*SE*, 157–58).

In an earlier essay Williams states: "We seek a language which will not be at least a deformation of speech as we know it—but will embody all the advantageous jumps, swiftnesses, colors, movements of the day—that will, at least, not exclude language as spoken—all language (present) as spoken" (*SE*, 109).

When Williams was asked in an interview in 1950 what makes the American language so different, he responded, "Well, our lives are lived according to a certain rhythm, whether we know it or not. There is a pace to our lives, which largely governs our lives. There's no question about it. You take a young man who is employed by Standard Oil. Well his

23. William Carlos Williams, "The American Idiom," *Fresco*, I (1960), 15, 16.

life is set to the pace of Standard Oil. . . . That's his pace, and
the language they speak is his language. . . . I take what I
find, I make a poem out of it" (*Int*, 24). Williams read "Ol'
Bunk's Bank" to the interviewer as an example of a poem
"with a lot of good American in it" (*Int*, 20–22).

Throughout his career Williams practiced a "natural" use of
the elements of style, vocabulary, syntax, and figurative language. He equated naturalness with the American idiom and
with everyday speech rhythms and vocabulary. But a concern
with diction, syntax, does not guarantee that there will be
movement to a poet's lines. Characters in poems from the
1930s would often just sit in Williams' verse.

> She sits with
> tears on
>
> her cheek
> her cheek on
>
> her hand
> the child
>
> in her lap
> his nose
>
> pressed
> to the glass ("Young Woman at a Window," *CEP*, 369)

Nothing moves but the attention. In the later poems, finding
themselves in lines that move, the characters can walk and explore the world; the measure gives stride.

> A Negro Woman
>
>   carrying a bunch of marigolds
>   wrapped
>   in an old newspaper:
>   She carries them upright,
>   bareheaded,
>   the bulk
>   of her thighs
>   causing her to waddle
>   as she walks. . . . (*PB*, 123)

The poem is a poem of process; now the poet has a vehicle to
embody his love of motion, of life.

According to Sherman Paul, who writes with great sensitivity of Williams' late poetry in *The Music of Survival*, Williams' shift in interest from image to motion was a result of his growing older, needing a longer line that would permit him to write in an autobiographical mode. "The autobiographical impulse," writes Paul, "usually arises in a late stage of life when one is concerned more for the continuity than the topography of the self."[24] Late poems such as "Asphodel" required new technique, longer lines with more internal variety, to permit Williams to express the time of memory, "duration."

In the 1940s Williams began to emphasize, or to reemphasize, the need for a new measure. But Williams' interest in meter, in the movement of his lines, was not new to the late poems or to his theoretical interests, though he may not have been able to accomplish the creation of the triadic line until the late 1940s. As early as 1913, Williams had been involved in a dialogue with Harriet Monroe at *Poetry* over the meter of his poem "Immortal." When Monroe called the meter "irregular," Williams objected to her dogmatism and asked, "Why not call it some other kind of a measure?" (*SL*, 24). He was already looking for a new measure, even though he did not know what to call it then (or even what to call the measure in 1948, when he made a breakthrough with his three-ply lines in *Paterson II*). In an early essay, "Speech Rhythm," dated 1913, Williams makes a full statement of his interest in the quality of motion in poetry.[25] Though it does not contain the word "measure," this essay contains some of Williams' clearest statements on his interest in the kinetics of the line. We will look at this statement in chapter 3, in order to help us understand the way the idea of "measure" is put into practice in "Asphodel."

Although Williams showed a theoretical interest in prosody early in his career, it would take him forty years of experimen-

24. Sherman Paul, *The Music of Survival: A Biography of a Poem by William Carlos Williams* (Urbana, 1968), 27.

25. Mike Weaver discovered this document uncatalogued among the Viola Baxter Jordan papers at the University of Connecticut. See Mike Weaver's *William Carlos Williams: The American Background* (Cambridge, England, 1971), 82–83.

tation to find the variable foot with a pattern of lines that was both flexible and ordered enough to suit his requirements for verse. Throughout his life Williams kept working at style. The triadic line, while it answered the need for a measure capable of expressing reflection and memory, also satisfied the need for a line that could include more of the experience of the world around us through its rhythm.

The triadic line, or verse unit of three lines, each of the same duration but composed of variable feet, was Williams' answer to the problem of finding a new measure. Williams had seen and admired the triadic line in Pound's translations of Cavalcanti, but his own use of the line in *Journey to Love* to explore the quality of love through memory is novel.[26]

The variable foot, Williams explains, "is simply what it describes itself to be: a poetic foot that is not fixed but varies with the demands of the language. . . ."[27] The number of syllables per foot or line may vary, depending on the poet's sense of the line's music. The beat or tempo is kept regular from line to line; as in classical verse the line is based on duration, on time elapsed, and not on stress or on a traditional count of syllables. Williams points out that Spanish poets of the seventeenth century preceded him in the use of "versos sueltos," or "loose verses."[28]

Denise Levertov, who as a young poet learned a great deal from Williams, explains her sense of Williams' discovery. "I think that what the idea of the variable foot, which is so difficult to understand, really depends on is a sense of pulse, a pulse in behind the words, a pulse that is actually sort of tapped out by a drum in the poem. Yes, there's an implied beat, and as in music, there is such a beat, and you can have in one bar just two notes, and in another bar you have, you know, ten notes, and yet the bar length is the same."[29] Williams

26. Williams, "Letter on Pound," 301.

27. William Carlos Williams, "The American Language Again," *Pound Newsletter*, VIII (October, 1955), 6.

28. Williams, "Letter on Pound," 301.

29. Denise Levertov, *Denise Levertov: In Her Own Province* (New York, 1979), 32.

thinks the variable foot is "simply what it describes," but Levertov sees the concept as a difficult one: the variable foot is not easy to accomplish; the new measure depends on the poet's having an excellent ear for cadences, for the beat.

It is likely that the variable foot is neither so rigidly ordered as to be measured by musical notation, nor as vague an entity as to be merely Williams' way of hearing verse.[30] In a letter to Richard Eberhart, Williams states that "by measure I mean musical pace." He tells Eberhart that he does not actually count the beats while writing, unless the count is done "half consciously . . . under my breath. . . ." But the lines are capable of being counted. Williams gives the following example from "Daphne and Virginia" (1954) to show how he counts his lines:

(1) The smell of the heat is boxwood
      (2) when rousing us
           (3) a movement of the air
(4) stirs our thoughts
      (5) that had no life in them
           (6) to a life, a life in which. . . . (*SL*, 326)

The reader is instructed to "count a single beat to each numeral. . . . Over the whole poem it gives a pattern to the meter that can be felt as a new measure" (*SL*, 327).

What the poet has done is to syncopate the lines according to a regular beat, with a varied number of syllables to each line. Each foot provides us with a sense of the continuing action of the poem, which in this case is to be "roused" and "stirred" to imaginative life, to speak of love. A breakthrough has been made in shifting reliance from an established meter to the poet's sense of rhythm; yet the poem does retain a sense of order through the regular if somewhat impressionistic count.

Williams first used the variable foot and three-ply line in 1948, in Book Two, Section III of *Paterson*. The section begins:

30. Hélène Dupeyron-Marchessou, *William Carlos Williams et le renouveau du lyrisme* (Paris, 1967), 192; John Malcolm Brinnin, *William Carlos Williams* (Minneapolis, 1963), 32–35.

> The descent beckons
>   as the ascent beckoned
>   Memory is a kind
> of accomplishment,
>   a sort of renewal
>   even. . . . (*P*, 96)

Out of the complexities of *Paterson*, with its many voices and an assortment of styles collected from contemporary life, with its tolerance for ambiguities and its sorrow at the blocks to our creative lives, the ordered, continuous song of the "Descent" rises effortlessly like a clear fountain from underground. Its music carries through to all the poems in *Journey to Love*. The "Descent" poem springs forth like a new season after the opening passage in Section III, which is both an invocation and a struggle with "that rule" that obliterates being. "But Spring shall come and flowers will bloom / and man must chatter of his doom" (*P*, 95).

In *I Wanted to Write a Poem* Williams refers to this stylistic innovation in *Paterson* as a "milestone," a "sea-change" (80, 83). Williams considered this form of line to be the major accomplishment of his career, though he admitted to Eberhardt, "I should have been more aware of it than I was. I did through my skin sense it, but for it to reach the level of consciousness should not have taken a lifetime" (*SL*, 329).

The poet spoke to Eberhardt of this passage from *Paterson* as "my solution of the problem of modern verse." And he predicted his continued exploration of the discovery: "As far as I know, as my forthcoming book makes clear, I shall use no other form for the rest of my life, for it represents the culmination of all my striving after an escape from the rigid restrictions of the verse of the past" (*SL*, 334). This statement is dated June 13, 1955, one of Williams' last entries in Thirlwall's *Collected Letters*. Indeed, Williams did use the triadic line and variable foot in the poems in *Journey to Love* (1955), including the poem "Asphodel" (then called "Work in Progress"). All of these poems appear in the collected late poems, *Pictures from Brueghel* (1962).

It is no coincidence that Williams' triadic lines also contain the theme of descent. It was as if Williams had been waiting for just such a tool in order to plunge more deeply into his materials. As Sherman Paul puts it, "The poem itself is an action of the imagination in its initiation or 'entering into.' This explains why formal invention, apart from its supreme cultural importance, means so much to Williams: with its help he develops and pursues the exploring self."[31]

Williams' years of work at his craft gave him the technical facility to be clear and simple, to choose his subject matter in his late years. In *Journey to Love*, in "Asphodel, That Greeny Flower," he chose to write above love, about memory and music, and to write without rhetoric.

The last poems "had to recreate a complete area of life; they had to present the 'complex as simple.'"[32] The triadic line enabled Williams to incorporate more of his experience than he could have done in earlier forms. J. Hillis Miller also recognizes this triumph of the late poems to include, to make the complex simple and particular: "To read *Paterson* or 'Asphodel, That Greeny Flower' is to enter into a region where everything the poet has ever experienced is present together, each item in its particularity ready to be called on when needed."[33] The new measure is a way for the poet to sum up. Williams' poetic development through his lifetime can be seen as a meditation and a working toward the measure that would permit him freedom, order, the greatest flexibility for moving in the late poems through the range and depths of his experiences.

Certainly Williams saw his career as a poet as vindicated by his work on structure, with measure as the key to structure. In all his writings on poetics Williams stresses that measure is of the utmost significance for the poem; there lies the realm of technical innovation that informs and satisfies the imagination. "To measure is all we know," the poet sings in *Paterson*

31. Paul, *The Music of Survival*, 20.
32. Linda Welshimer Wagner, *The Poems of William Carlos Williams: A Critical Study* (Middletown, Conn., 1963, 1964), 124.
33. J. Hillis Miller, *Poets of Reality*, 303.

(*P*, 277). In "The Poem as a Field of Action" Williams insists, "The only reality we can know is measure. . . ." The structure of the poem reflects the "social, economic complex of the world at any time" (*SE*, 283). Measure reflects contemporary truths and values. In a letter to John Thirlwall, Williams asserts, "To measure is all a human being can do with the world—Poetry is . . . Measure."[34] The line breaks, the rhythm of the poem, are ways of knowing and exploring the world about us. The transposition of the pace of our lives into the rhythm of the poem is an act of consciousness, according to Williams, a taking stock of our position in a world in process.

Williams builds on the concept and metaphors of measure throughout his writings. Early in Williams' writings, in the letter to Harriet Monroe, the word "measure" is both a literal way of speaking of the meter of the poem and a way of registering his dissatisfaction with traditional prosody.

The contemporary measure must reflect the pace and the essence of our own lives and break the hold of the "medieval masterbeat"[35] imposed by the traditional line. If the new measure is contemporary, it is also very old, ancient in its origins; contemporary poetics involves a rediscovery of a measure based on time, rather than on stress. The measure, "the movement in words," is a rhythmic communication that to the Greeks and to Williams "meant as much or more than the words themselves."[36] Measure, the rhythmic base of the poem, is movement and order, a generative activity of mind as well as "something measured" (*SE*, 340).

Measure, Williams reminds us, originates in dance, in a pace informed by the body and heartbeat. "We are reminded that the origin of our verse was the dance and even if it had not been the dance, the heart when it is stirred has multiple beats, and verse at its most impassioned sets the heart violently beating. But as the heart picks up we also begin to

34. John Thirlwall, "The Last Poems of William Carlos Williams," in *New Directions in Prose and Poetry: 16* (New York, 1956), 26.
35. William Carlos Williams, "The American Spirit in Art," *American Academy of Arts and Letters Proceedings*, 2nd Ser., II (1952), 59.
36. "Briarcliff Junior College Talk," 12.

count. Finally, the measure for each language and environment is accepted."[37]

Music is also a source for Williams' thoughts on measure. His first encounter with "Measure" in a "wholly musical context" was his reading of the "Varia" section of *Antheil and the Treatise on Harmony*.[38] There, Williams would have read that the "instinctive" musician comprehends the "shape of things" in music.[39] Louis Zukofsky, with whom Williams worked on Objectivist poetry in the 1930s, continued to call the metrical patterns of his verse "musical shapes."[40] Zukofsky's search for a counterpart to a Bach fugue in his poetry calls to mind Williams' reference to the lines of "Asphodel" as "fugal music."[41]

But poetry for Williams is not music, any more than it is science, though poetry may assimilate metaphors and ideas of space and time from both. Poetry has its own inner music, or rhythmic speech. "By its *music* shall the best of modern verse be known and the *resources* of the music." The new measure results "in a language which we hear spoken about us every day" (*SL*, 326–27).

With the sensitive register of his verse the modern poet measures the pace of speech; in the placement of his words and lines the poet measures words with the skill of an astrophysicist studying the stars. Measure is the gauge and also what is measured; the mind looks with precision at the shapes consciousness takes and changes itself as it measures.

> Without invention nothing is well spaced,
> unless the mind change, unless
> the stars are new measured, according
> to their relative positions, the

37. ELG, 39. Also quoted by Jerome Mazzaro, *William Carlos Williams: The Later Poems* (Ithaca, 1973), 26–27.
38. Mike Weaver, *William Carlos Williams: The American Background* (Cambridge, England, 1971), 68.
39. *Antheil and the Treatise on Harmony, with Supplementary Notes by Ezra Pound* (Chicago, 1927), 131.
40. Weaver, *William Carlos Williams*, 66.
41. "The River of Heaven," 21 (Worksheets, typed copy for section III of "Asphodel," YALC).

> line will not change, the necessity
> will not matriculate: unless there is
> a new mind there cannot be a new
> line. . . .   (*P*, 65)

In the late essay, Williams describes the development of a new measure as "a moral gesture." The contemporary poem requires a realignment in structure to reflect the truths of our present experience: "it is the measure which is the objective, a change in the measure, which most affect our lives." The change is a moral act, in that American writers assert the validity of their own style of life. "To measure our lives after the accepted style of English prosody which we are still taught in our universities and to which our moral codes are still made, unacknowledged, made to fit explains how deep the fissure, or fission, goes." It is a "moral risk" we take when we explore and measure our own experience, our own world, with words. Measure implies depth for Williams; pacing and rhythm go deeper than words, "deeper than that, the measure of our lines, the way they are deployed on the page goes for us deepest of all."[42]

Williams goes on to state that words have nothing to do with the "American idiom." "To make such a statement seems absurd," he acknowledges. "What else is verse made of but 'word, words, words?' Quite literally, the spaces between the words, in our modern understanding, which takes with them an equal part in the measure." "Where are we to turn? to measure, a reassurance of a new measure. The literary world has been closed to us from our birth by the past. The discovery of a new continent has the connotation of a new continent in the world of literature also."[43]

"Verse is measure . . ." (*SE*, 212) and measure is all of the meanings the term accumulated through Williams' writings. Measure is count, beat, rhythmic pace, freedom and order, a way of gauging, a way of knowing, discipline, discovery. That

---

42. "Measure: —a loosely assembled essay," 61, 55, 56, 56, 57.
43. *Ibid.*, 58, 64.

Williams did not say all of these things at once does not mean that he did not finally know what measure was. In his poetry Williams lets his images accrue meanings from poem to poem, gathering metaphorical significance. Like the image of the flower in his poetry, the term "measure" gathers its meanings through the repeated statement of his theoretical discoveries. Williams was content to use the term "measure" as long as the word was fruitful and continued to attract meaning. "Asphodel, That Greeny Flower" blossoms as the fulfillment of Williams' meditation on the new measure.

Of interest to us in understanding Williams' greatness as a poet is his attitude toward his search for technical innovations, his faith in a new poetry even when he had no clear form to rely on. In a letter to Kay Boyle, 1932, Williams refers to the time they live in as a "formless interim" for poetry. "For myself, I have written little poetry," he says. "Form, the form has been lacking. Instead I have been watching speech in my own environment . . ." (*SL*, 129). Williams relies on "the seriousness of poetry itself" (*SL*, 133) as a beginning, an attitude that will lead to the new form that poetry must have. He begins in this letter to talk about the line: "The line must, as a minimum, have a well-conceived form within which modification may exist." The poet is guessing what the new line will be like, but he knows "one more positive thing though— or minimal requisite. It seems to me that the 'foot' being at the bottom of all prosody, the time has come when that must be recognized to have changed in nature. And it must be seen to have changed in its rhythmical powers of inclusion" (*SL*, 136). Williams wrote this in 1932, sixteen years before he discovered a flexible line.

In a letter to Parker Tyler in 1946, Williams also indicates patience, a willingness to wait while reaching for the new formal discovery that he knows will take place. Williams tells Tyler that he had just been lecturing on Paul Eluard, on "verbal design," when he was questioned from the audience as to whether he himself had written anything in the "new way of measuring." Williams relates to Tyler that "it was a fair question but one I shall have to postpone answering indefinitely. I always think of Mendelejeff's table of atomic weights in this connection. Years before an element was discovered, the element helium, for instance, its presence had been predicated by a blank in the table of atomic weights." Williams is not sure that he is the poet to fulfill his own predictions for a new form, but he knows that "the innovation I predict must come to be" (*SL*, 243).

Surely Williams' capacity to wait in formlessness while reaching toward the new form was part of his genius. His patience and clairvoyant expectation enabled him to work hard, while extending antennae toward new formal possibilities. Here is an attitude of "Preparedness" or "simply 'Awakeness,'" a mood of concentrated anticipation that is one of the "virtues a musician can develop," especially if he or she works with improvisation.[44] Among Williams' letters to Cid Corman, dated 1955, we find a handwritten note that the poet seems to have scribbled both to Corman and to himself: "When one blazes a path—it is unrecognizable until you have yourself gone over it."[45]

Not that the critics cared. Among other obstacles that he had to overcome, Williams had to write for most of his life without the approval or interest of the critics. In his letters we find references to his poems' being "buried" (*SL*, 257); Williams himself felt that he was being buried like Persephone in hell.

The first part of *Paterson* (1946) had been misunderstood by the critics as formless. Williams responds in a letter,

Poetry, an art, is what answer I have. My poetry appears to most as formless, to the neo-orthodox as an offense to be safely ignored. The God-damned fools. That's why I despise the crew. . . .

I fight with Blackmur, I feel resentments against them all, and all I can do (growing old) is to compose. It is the only recourse, the only

44. Cornelius Cardew, "Virtues That a Musician Can Develop," *I-Kon*, I (1968), 19.
45. William Carlos Williams, in a handwritten note included among letters to Cid Corman, 1953–1956, HRHRC.

intellectual recourse for an artist, to make, to make, to make, and to go on making—*never* to reply *in kind* to their strictures. (*SL*, 238)

The history of the critics' relationship to Williams and his work is a history of ignorance, misunderstanding, and indifference.[46] Yvor Winters was probably one of Williams' most consistently vicious critics; his attacks on Williams seem to have had more to do with his prejudices about what poetry should be and about his own stature than with any kind of attempt to read Williams' work. In 1965, in response to a query by J. Hillis Miller as to whether his opinion of Williams' writing had changed over the years, Winters picked out a few "minor poems" that he thought were successful and then "offered his final dismissal: 'To say that Williams was anti-intellectual would be almost an exaggeration: he did not know what the intellect was.'"[47]

With such a comment in mind, we should not be surprised to learn from one of Williams' letters to Beum in 1950 that the poet directed some of his theoretical writings to Winters. Williams writes:

Ivor Winters is NOT in sympathy with what we are trying to do. He WAS in sympathy when he and I corresponded on the subject 20 or 30 years ago but he changed his mind. He changed his mind violently and positively rejected my viewpoint—and went in the opposite direction.

The "theory" mentioned above [Williams refers here to a 1950 statement on "The Measure"] is largely addressed to Ivor Winters—tho' I would not care to say so. What would be the use? . . . It couldn't possibly help us. We have a job to do. When it is done—if it ever gets done his answer will be served to him. . . .[48]

To a certain extent, Williams may have developed his theoretical views in response to Winters, just as he "forced himself to be successful" at his poetry in response to Eliot. Yet de-

46. See Mariani's study, *William Carlos Williams: The Poet and His Critics*, for a complete history of critical responses to the poet's work.
47. *Ibid.*, 59.
48. William Carlos Williams to R. Beum, January 9, 1950 (uncatalogued, UB).

spite his best efforts to fight back against obstacles creatively, Williams saw the lack of understanding, the lack of serious attention from the critics, as a hindrance to his career, to his work as a poet. As he stated in a late interview, "A writer's success can definitely be hurt by obscurity if it is judged by popularity or income. Critics often get down on such a man and hurt his reputation." Characteristically, Williams adds, "But if he is a real writer, he will keep on. I never had an audience until I was past fifty. But I wrote all the time anyway. I had to" (*Int*, 30–31).

Critical approval came only in the late years, and it helped Williams to write with the calm and assured tone that we find in "Asphodel, That Greeny Flower." With Flossie's understanding and the sureness that he found in the new measure, Williams could go forward in the late poems to apply the American idiom in a new way. He could bring to bear his directness, his natural speech rhythms, on a journey into memory and self-discovery. The triadic line, the longer line, covered the space of experience Whitman might have covered. But Williams' lines, syncopated and disciplined now, enable the poet to voyage—in hell's despite—into his extraordinary love song.

Part II

OF ASPHODEL

CHAPTER THREE

Conversation as Design

One way Williams manages to make his extended poem "Asphodel, That Greeny Flower" sound simple and direct is by creating a tone of intimacy. The speaker in the poem, the aging poet Williams, talks directly to his wife as if he were speaking to himself. He appeals to his wife's understanding and generosity:

> I call on you
>   as I do on myself the same
>   to forgive. . . . (*PB*, 175)

It is remarkable that Williams can sustain an atmosphere of intimacy throughout a thirty-page poem, one that includes references to other works of art from Homer to Rimbaud. This modern confessional poem has epic qualities; it includes cultural figures and historical notes in the way that Pound's *Cantos* is inclusive, or in the way that Joyce's *Ulysses* manages to include a world in its story. "Asphodel" covers the epic space of the seas, but "seen" through the bones and body of the aging bard, Williams; covers a deep vertical space or "stem" in its mythic journey to the depths of memory. Chaos, the sea, has been ruled for the moment by the measure of the poet's love, and "the sea . . . sways / peacefully upon its plantlike stem" (*CEP*, 87). "Asphodel" tells a story of renewed love in old age. But within the poet's account of his relearning to love, he includes an interweaving of various thematic strands or leitmotifs. The narrative is more circular than linear, moving from an address to Flossie, out to an examination of self in the world and of the world's history, back to Flossie again. The poem becomes a symphony, a world with its complexities, yet "Asphodel" is primarily a personal lyric because of its tone. Intimacy provides a unity of effect; the poem is a gift for Flossie: "I bring you / a last flower" (*PB*, 178).

Epic poets in the heroic age of Greece were credited with "qualities of memory and vision" that enabled them to "rescue the past from oblivion, restoring it to life and moving their hearers to pity and fear."[1] Williams wants to rescue his past with Flossie, to restore their love, and move her to pity and love. Through the story of their love's renewal "every man / who wants to die at peace in his bed" will learn of the power of the imagination (*PB*, 162). The song is launched with an inverted phrase that calls to mind the opening line of *The Aeneid*. Yet instead of "arms and the man" Williams sings "to you" "of asphodel," the "greeny," ghostly flower of memory. He turns the impulse for war into a journey to love; he wills this new beginning with a mythical flower, made delicate and personal in his song.

The effect of embracing a modern epic within the lyric, personal voice is to make the world personal for the reader, to create the "human universe" that Charles Olson spoke of in his essay by that name.[2] The poet or reader who is intimate with his or her feelings, whose response to the world begins at the skin, feels a connection to others and to the world. He or she cannot treat the world as refuse. Williams deliberately refers to the threat of the atom bomb within his love poem—

1. Seymour M. Pitcher, "Epic. Theory," in Alex Preminger, Frank J. Warnke, and O. B. Hardison, Jr. (eds.), *Princeton Encyclopedia of Poetry and Poetics* (Princeton, 1965), 242.

2. "Art does not seek to describe but to enact. And if man is once more to possess intent in his life, and to take up the responsibility implicit in his life, he has to comprehend his own process as intact, from outside, by way of his skin, in, and by his own powers of conversion, out again." Charles Olson, "Human Universe," *Human Universe and Other Essays* (New York, 1967), 10.

the bomb is there as a warning against the impersonal. Like Anaïs Nin, for whom Williams felt an affinity,[3] Williams speaks with the conviction that the personal voice, the particular voice, is responsible for the world:

> To make a start,
> out of particulars
> and make them general. . . . (*P*, 11)

Williams involves the reader through direct address: "I come, my sweet, / to sing to you" (*PB*, 153). Here the poet sings to his wife but establishes a connection with the reader as well, makes the reader into a friend. Baudelaire also implicates the reader by means of direct address: "Tu le connais, lecteur . . . / —Hypocrite lecteur, —mon semblable, —mon frère!"[4] But Williams' tone is one of tenderness, not derision. If the English "you" could be divided into the formal "you" (*vous*) and the familiar "you" (*tu*), Williams would be using the familiar form—without any of Baudelaire's bitter sarcasm. Williams and his wife are "semblables," equals, because they have lived long together, and Williams will create his readers into equals by sharing his experience with them. The poet and his readers are "innocent of heart" in this collaboration, this attempt to oppose the creations of the imagination against death's destroying powers. Williams cannot afford to be a hypocrite in "Asphodel," for the poem is a death song, a song of resoluteness and affirmation in the face of death. Williams' song is a test and a proof of his having existed; he sings as a tribal warrior would sing.

> Let us see, is this real
> Let us see, is this real
> This life I am living.[5]

The poems in *Journey to Love* test the existence and sustaining power of love.

3. William Carlos Williams, "Men . . . Have No Tenderness," *New Directions: 7* (Norfolk, Conn., 1942), 429–36.
4. Charles Baudelaire, *Oeuvres complètes* (Paris, 1961), 6.
5. John Bierhorst (ed.), *In the Trail of the Wind: American Indian Ritual Poems and Ritual Orations* (New York, 1971), 131.

> . . . I love you
> or I do not live
> at all. ("The Ivy Crown," *PB*, 124)

Williams relies on the strength of personal pronouns throughout the poem. Though he addresses his wife, Flossie, as "you,"
he never uses her name in the poem. The poem is particular,
special, "to you / and you alone," but not exclusive; the poet
involves the reader in his strategy of intimacy. Williams repeats himself, with a purpose.

> There is something
> something urgent
> I have to say to you
> and you alone. . . . (*PB*, 154)

The repetition of "to you" creates the effect of establishing a
direct line to the wife, but also to the feminine element within
the poet's self. The poet knows that there is a creative and mer-
ciful feminine principle within his voice.

> I do not come to you
> save that I confess
> to being
> half man and half
> woman. ("For Eleanor and Bill Monahan," *PB*, 84)

Often the "you" in "Asphodel" is used as the object of a prepo-
sition, to bring the poet nearer to his wife, or to the feminine.

> It is a curious odor,
> a moral odor,
> that brings me
> near to you. (*PB*, 155)

Through prepositions used with pronouns the poet can approach his wife with the gift of the poem and with his way of
seeing. Twice, he says, "I come, my sweet, / to sing to you"
(*PB*, 153, 161).

The poet continues to involve his wife and the reader
through the use of a question to the listener, again, directed
familiarly to "you."

We danced,
in our minds,
and read a book together.
You remember? (*PB*, 157–58)

"Asphodel" is composed of three books and a coda. In Book I alone the poet uses the pronoun "you" twenty-three times. The result of the repetition is to assert the poet's need for intimacy with his wife, to reaffirm their connection.

Williams relies on the pronoun "we" to emphasize what he and his wife, or he and his listeners, have shared. The wife is asked to will an acknowledgment of shared experience.

We lived long together
a life filled,
if you will,
with flowers. (*PB*, 153)

Bill and Flossie lived in Rutherford, not far from the ocean; metaphorically they were born as a couple by exploring the common landscape of their experience,

for we were born by the sea,
knew its rose hedges
to the very water's brink. (*PB*, 156)

The couple will live on together in memory, signified by the wedding scene at the end of the poem. "Asphodel" covers distance, the distance to the "water's very brink," the time of aging together, and the inner time of shared memories.

Possessive pronouns add to the bond that the poet is establishing. His seeing and his feeling touch the eyes of his beloved.

What do I remember
that was shaped
as this thing is shaped?
while our eyes fill
with tears. (*PB*, 153)

"Our eyes" refers not only to that which the poet and his wife share in their seeing, but to the seeing that the poet gives the reader.

The extensive use of pronouns to bind the lyric structure as well as the desire to create a shared language reminds us of Paul Eluard's love poetry. Through the use of pronouns, Eluard too made the world habitable, a shared place, illuminated by song.

> The lamp is filled with our eyes
> We inhabit our valley
> Our walls our flowers our sun
> Our colors and our light
>
> The capital of the sun
> Is in our image
> And in the shelter of our walls
> Our door is a human door. ("By a Kiss")[6]

Williams knew early in his career that he wanted to break down barriers between poet and reader. "Whenever I say, 'I' I mean also, 'you'. And so, together, as one, we shall begin," Williams writes in 1923 (*I*, 89). The poet seeks a common language, one his readers can share. The poet's attitude of collaborating with the reader creates a different kind of reader from the merely objective critic—Williams seeks a reader who is willing to experience the immediacy and truth of feeling in his language. J. Hillis Miller takes an extreme position on the relationship of Williams and the critic. "To accept the embrace Williams offers means the impossibility of 'criticizing' his work, if criticism means viewing with the cold eye of analysis and judgment. The critic must resign himself to the poet's world and accept whatever he finds there."[7] Williams would have disagreed; there is no reason why the reader cannot examine Williams' work with a critical eye, since Williams himself worked so hard on design. Williams hoped that readers after him would understand subtleties in his work that he himself could not as yet describe. But there is more to a critical reading of the poem than analysis; to be a partner with the poet

6. Paul Eluard, *Last Love Poems*, trans. Marilyn Kallet (Baton Rouge, 1980), 2–3.
7. J. Hillis Miller, *Poets of Reality: Six Twentieth Century Writers* (Cambridge, Mass., 1966), 291.

in the language of the poem, the reader has to allow his or her imagination to play over the grid of words, to suspend disbelief for a time. Williams would have wanted his work to stand up under the cold eye of critical judgment, as long as the critics had done him the justice of understanding his design.

In "The Simplicity of Disorder" (1921–1931) Williams had begun to meditate upon a poem with "conversation as design," conversation between husband and wife. The poet speaks to himself as he imagines the design.

> By this singleness do you, my dear, become actually my wife.
> By design do you become bright, purely what you are (and visible), not to bear me a message—but as a wife you carry me the freshness of all women. There is no necessity for witty fingers. The solidity of the pure lends itself by pure design in which you are accomplished.
> That would be a writing.
> What's that?
> In which conversation was actual to the extent that it would be pure design.
> How?
> Till death do us part. (*SE*, 98)

In "Asphodel" love for Flossie is transposed into the "pure design" of the triadic line and the variable foot; her presence becomes actual through the song. The fact that the poem may be conceived of objectively, as a design, does not detract from its effect as a statement of emotion. In a late interview Williams spoke of his goal in writing "Asphodel." "My main aim is to break up the usual metric pattern. In order to get away from the conventional thing, dividing it by breath, by inflection. I wanted to get away from everything that is English" (*Int*, 68). He believed, in fact, that the form of his poem would itself generate a response. "When you are emotionally stirred . . . you speak with the emotions. . . . We want a familiar pattern, a 'home' pattern to bring the conviction out in the listener."[8] In "Asphodel" the poet's measure syncopates natural speech rhythms with the ebb and flow of imaginative seas,

8. William Carlos Williams, "Talk about Poetry," March 28, 1954. On tape at the Rutherford Free Public Library.

with the "inner voice,"[9] the voice of memory. The triadic line and variable foot punctuate the poem with a regular beat that does not distort the pace and flow of the American idiom; the reader feels at home in Williams' language.

That Williams did not get away from "everything English" is obvious in his use of Spenserian phrases of song. But the measure, the cuts that give the poem character, the swiftness of pace that propels it along, is Williams' "local" pattern that assimilates British prosody for its own uses (for the poem's love of pageantry). Williams assimilates Spenser to enrich the American poem, the way Spenser had assimilated words and rhythms from Italian and other European languages to enrich the English language. The naturalness of American speech patterns dominates "Asphodel's" song. "Asphodel" is a dialogue with the past and with the future of poetry.

On one rough-draft copy of "Asphodel," found in the Yale Collection, Williams wrote "a dialogue" at the top of the poem, in pencil and in brackets. Perhaps he was referring to his earlier thought of a "conversation as design." Perhaps he thought of the poem as creating a sense of closeness and connecting voices, "a reciprocal language," as Paul Eluard put it, where poet and reader could share a common language of love. The poem would include the syntax and cadences of conversation to make its lines direct. As we can see, the final version does not include Flossie's part of the conversation. The poet's speaking is Flossie's speaking; her listening is all the participating she gets to do, at least in the poem. Perhaps the poet meant the poem to be something of a dialogue with himself, a meditation on love and wholeness in the manner of Stevens' "The World as Meditation" or "The Final Soliloquy of the Interior Paramour."[10] In any case, he erased the reference to "a dialogue" in the final version.

Book II of the poem is both more sombre and more wide-reaching than the first book. "Approaching death," perhaps "the death of love" as well, the poet meditates on his place in

9. Denise Levertov, *Denise Levertov: In Her Own Province* (New York, 1979), 33.
10. Wallace Stevens, *Poems* (New York, 1959), 163–64, 157–58.

history, on the treacheries and discoveries in history and in modern times. The modern poem is a dance, reflecting universal concerns through the modern measure. But "the bomb puts an end / to all that" (*PB*, 165). The use of fewer personal pronouns in this section, the reliance on "I" rather than "you" or "we" throughout most of this book, corresponds to the devastating thought of the bomb, created by those who cannot imagine the existence of others. In this book the poet surveys his losses and the world's losses through war's destruction of art. The book ends with the poet's greatest sense of loss, the loss of his capacity to create shared words: "I regret most— / that there has come an end / to them." Book II is a canto concerned with fragmentation and endings; though it contains memories of "pinnacles" of personal history, the book is also a deliberate facing of death (*PB*, 169).

Book III begins with a renewed appeal to the other, the "you" of the poem: "What power has love but forgiveness?" (*PB*, 169). Having been shown the shattering effects of the bomb, of lovelessness, Flossie is called upon to heal the poet's sense of a fragmented world through her love. The wife is like the imagination itself—she can restore his spirits.

> You have forgiven me
>   making me new again.
>   So that here
> in the place
>   dedicated in the imagination
>   to memory
> of the dead
>   I bring you
>   a last flower. (*PB*, 177–78)

Having given the gift of understanding, the wife receives the gift of the poem, which is the best that Williams can give, a poem ruled by love.

Yet in this section Williams voyages outside of Flossie's domestic realm. Entering the depths of subways and caves, the poet makes contact not only with the image of his father and the fathers of art, but with the image of the Venus in prehistoric caves. His love carries him back to the eternal femi-

nine principle, to Demeter or Kore, to the "big buttocked" figures of the Great Mother. By "sympathetic magic," by contact
with "his father's beard," the poet seems to move effortlessly
in an archaic landscape. His "draftsmanship" permits him to
imagine a world beyond the personal, to "build a picture of all
men." Then humbly he returns home, to thoughts of Flossie
"compassionately pouring at the roots" of her plants. Not
Rhea or Demeter, goddesses of vegetation and grain, but
Flossie is *actually* with him, "moved by kindness" to warm
and care for him (*PB*, 174–75).

The "Coda" (*PB*, 178) at the end of the poem sings of light,
the mind's light, celebrated through the image of a wedding.
The mind is at peace with itself; the marriage of art and life
has taken place through the poem's evocation of memories.
Williams watches the light of his lines rhythmically stroke the
"floor" of the page, as Mrs. Ramsay in *To the Lighthouse*
watched the lighthouse beams bend across the marriage bed
and stroke the floor. Like Mrs. Ramsay, the poet experiences a
growing tenderness or generous pity toward others as toward
himself in the steady light of his seeing. In *To the Lighthouse*
Mrs. Ramsay's contemplative mind meets with itself in a
wedding: "There rose, and she looked and looked with her
needles suspended, there curled up off the floor of the mind,
rose from the lake of one's being, a mist, a bride to meet her
lover."[11] Williams, like this fictional Mrs. Ramsay, also "celebrates the light" of wholeness of mind, as much as he celebrates his love for Flossie.

Light or love, or the imagination, is wedded to speech in the
pageantry of the poem; light triumphs.

> The light
>   for all time shall outspeed
>   the thunder crack. (*PB*, 181)

Light is made personal at the end of the poem, for the poet's
memory shines on the details of his wedding to Flossie. He
returns to the particular, to the image of Flossie.

11. Virginia Woolf, *To the Lighthouse* (New York, 1965), 98.

```
At the altar
                so intent was I
    before my vows,
                so moved by your presence
                      a girl so pale
    and ready to faint
                that I pitied
                      and wanted to protect you. (PB, 181)
```

Light, the imagination, takes on an odor, becomes sensual.

```
                It is late
      but an odor
            as from our wedding
                  has revived for me. . . . (PB, 182)
```

Flossie's marriage to Williams, a "sweet-scented flower" (*PB*, 182), did blossom and enable the poet to create, to add light to the world with his creations; "the palm goes / always to the light" (*PB*, 180). Through the imagination the marriage of the poet and his wife has been transposed into the light or "pure design" of the poem. Now, Williams turns the imagination back to the immediate world again, offers the poem as a sensual reality to the reader.

Williams keeps the vocabulary of the poem simple. Monosyllabic words often prevail; ordinary words bear the gifts, *are* the gifts of songs, flowers.

```
      I come, my sweet,
                to sing to you.
    We lived long together
          a life filled,
                if you will,
      with flowers. (PB, 153)
```

Williams avoids affections of speech in his poetry. In Book III he speaks out against affectation.

```
                It is ridiculous
      what airs we put on
            to seem profound
                  while our hearts
      gasp dying
            for want of love. (PB, 170)
```

Poetry is speech, natural speech, for Williams. He sings of love in the American idiom. Poetry is an act of communication, of reaching out toward a listener, as the poet reaches out for understanding in "Asphodel." "Hear me out," he asks, simply (*PB*, 156).

The poet's use of a "general simple" vocabulary "makes certain words leap out in contrast." [12] In the first line of the poem "Of Asphodel, That Greeny Flower" (*PB*, 153) the word "asphodel" is curious, because it gives the reader a specific name of a flower. Though the flower itself may be common enough to find, the name has an uncommon sound to it. The long "o" sound chimes later in the poem in assonance with "forebodingly," to create a gloomy effect. (One thinks of Poe's description of how he composed "The Raven." Entranced by the beauty of melancholy subjects, Poe thought that the word "nevermore" seemed promising as a beginning, with its long "o," its melancholy sound effect.) [13] Yet "asphodel" also has a "del" sound (or dell within it); the word unfolds through a landscape evocative both of sorrow and of the fields of a pastoral landscape. The word "greeny" in the first line stands out; it picks up the tone from "asphodel" to a lighter, happier sound and reinforces the suggestion of a pastoral world. Though the word "greeny" is simple, it is a made-up word. The reader has to ponder its meaning. "Greeny" suggests a fertile, rolling place, suggests the sea; "asphodel," a white flower that Williams remembers from his childhood and from the underworld of Homer's *Odyssey*, comes from a personal, and a deep, universal place. Thus "asphodel" and "greeny" link suggestions of life and death together in the first line; as we will see, the poem has to it the quality of a living imagination moving among ghosts. The reader who is familiar with Williams' work will remember his line from "Celebration": "Time is a green orchid" (*CEP*, 190). Both "green" and "flowering" have for Williams associations with time.

12. Peter Meinke, "William Carlos Williams: Traditional Rebel," in Jerome Mazzaro (ed.), *Profile of William Carlos Williams* (Columbus, Ohio, 1971), 10.
13. Edgar Allan Poe, "First Principles," in Robert L. Hough (ed.), *Literary Criticism of Edgar Allan Poe* (Lincoln, 1965), 20–32.

The most unusual word in the poem is "guerdon." The poet is speaking about love, and says,

> Death
> > is not the end of it.
> There is a hierarchy
> > which can be attained,
> > > I think,
> in its service.
> > Its guerdon
> > > is a fairy flower;
> a cat of twenty lives. (*PB*, 157)

The word "guerdon" is a hybrid, between Middle English, Old French, Middle Latin sources (*guerdon, guerredon*, modified by Latin *donum*, "gift"); and the Old High German *widarlon* from *widar*, "against," and *lon*, "reward."[14] "Guerdon" brings to the poem a "rumor" of medieval pageantry, which, Williams reminds us in the "Coda," we so enjoy (*PB*, 81). The ceremony, a renewal of vows in the poem, is a gift for Flossie; the poem itself is a gift to the community. Williams only hints at his role of "knight in shining armor"—the unicorn and its pageantry belong to *Paterson V*, not to "Asphodel." Here the poet comes to be forgiven by his wife. As to the result of his entreaty, we can tell only that the poem receives the "guerdon," the reward of its enduring images. The poet is a "cat" with only one life, not nine or "twenty," though he had temporarily escaped death by surviving a few bouts with illnesses.

For Williams, the gift of the poem, written in the service of the imagination, has also to it a quality of warding off evil. In "The Desert Music" the formless, embryonic life-in-death image of the beggar does this "warding off" of endings; the accompanying imaginative music in the poet's lines is called "a protecting music." In "Asphodel" the image of the flower protects against meaninglessness; throughout his poetry Williams uses the flower as a "shield" against darkness, the way Aeneas uses the golden bough in *The Iliad*. The flower image is Williams' way of traveling through dangerous realms; for him the flower is a comfort and a protection. The image of the flower

14. *Oxford English Dictionary* (Oxford, 1933), 486.

has become for Williams his own emblem for his craft, his way of depicting an escape from death through the imagination.

In "The Yellow Flower" Williams refers to the common mustard flower as a curing flower, a "sacred flower" (*PB*, 89). Just as Michelangelo used marble, made it "bloom" as a way of exerting an immortal power, so the poet sees

>   through the eyes
>   and through the lips
>   and tongue the power
>   to free myself
>   and speak of it, as
>   Michelangelo through his hands
>   had the same, if greater,
>   power.

The poet has no marble, only

>   the tortured body of my flower
>   which is not a mustard flower at all
>   but some unrecognized
>   and unearthly flower. . . . (*PB*, 91)

The flower image for Williams provides "a hole / in the bottom of the bag," through which "we escape" death (*P*, 247).

The "fairy flower," or "guerdon," may also refer to the precious flower of immortality sought by Gilgamesh and Enkidu in Sumerian mythology. Gilgamesh lost the flower in a deep lake after a long quest.[15] For Williams, who also knows that he will lose, that death is inevitable; the flower represents art's power.

>   If no one came to try it
>   the world
>   would be the loser. (*PB*, 157)

Another technique that Williams uses in "Asphodel" to attain a striking effect of directness and immediacy is to make simple statements. His commands, or appeals, add a tone of urgency to the poem. "Hear me out. / Do not turn away," Williams insists, speaking in his own voice (*PB*, 156–57).

These lines remind us of an earlier poem, where Williams

15. Norma Lorre Goodrich (ed.), *Ancient Myths* (New York, 1960), 23.

depicts a woman as coy, attempting to keep her lover with her for a while longer. In "Two Pendants: for the Ears," Williams says his thoughts are

> like
> the distant smile of a woman who
> will say:
> —only to keep you a moment
> longer. Oh I know I'm a stinker—
> but
> only to keep you, it's only
> to keep you . a few moments
> Let me have a cigarette. (*CLP*, 218)

In his old age, Williams cannot afford to be coy in his plea for love and for time. ("I love you / or I do not live / at all.")

Time threatens Williams with death, as it threatens the world with its "flower," the bomb (*PB*, 165). Williams conveys a sense of immediacy as he speaks of

> . . . something
> something urgent
> I have to say to you. . . .

But even speech must wait, as the poet appreciates his wife's approach,

> but it must wait
> while I drink in
> the joy of your approach
> perhaps for the last time. (*PB*, 154)

Williams plays on our feelings here, letting his wife and the reader know that they should not deny the poet his last statement; they should appreciate what he will say.

Despite the directness and sense of resolve in Williams' tone, there is an undercurrent of precariousness and vulnerability. When the poet asks his wife not to turn away, he is reminding us of Book V of *The Aeneid*, where Aeneas appeals to Dido in the underworld: "Don't move away! Oh, let me see you a little longer! / To fly from me, when this is the last word fate allows us!" [16] There is an echo of sorrow, of tragedy in Wil-

---

16. Virgil, *The Aeneid of Virgil*, trans. C. Day Lewis (New York, 1953), 143.

liams' lines, evoked through the reference to the ancient story
of ill-fated lovers who, even in hell, had limited time.

Almost all of the lines of Williams' personal epic are made
of sentences whose syntax is regular and straightforward.
The sentences are syncopated by the triadic line. There are
narrative passages, which read like ordinary speech.

> When I was a boy
>> I kept a book
>>> to which, from time
> to time,
>> I added pressed flowers
>>> until, after time,
> I had a good collection. (*PB*, 155)

There are no distortions of speech or sentence structure in
Williams' lines. Instead, Williams uses the "cadences discoverable in prose" but imposes the regular beat and shape of
the triadic line. The result is to spin out the story, to place emphasis in this passage on "time" and to effect the simple "hop-
ping" cadence of a boy playing toward his destiny.

Sometimes the poet will slow down or even drag out the
pace of his verse, to indicate that he is stalling for time in his
words. Speech is his only weapon against his annihilation.

> And so
>> with fear in my heart
>>> I drag it out
> and keep on talking
>> for I dare not stop.
>>> Listen while I talk on
> against time. (*PB*, 154)

As the poet "talks on against time" we feel the pressure of
time bearing down on him. Williams repeats the word "time"
six times on pages 154–55; the repetition shows us the poet's
concerns. The writing in "Asphodel" is not hurried, does not
have the nervous rhythm of Williams' early poems, but is
paced, measured, through the variable foot and the triadic
line. The longer line length holds off terror, holds off death for
a time. The measure works as a strategy for the poet to keep
his beat regular. Memory holds off the pressure of time, for

                    Memory is a kind
        of accomplishment,
                a sort of renewal
            even. (*PB*, 73)

Song puts off time, too, for the music of love makes us forget
the "sorry facts" of mortality: "Of love, abiding love / it will be
telling" in the poet's song (*PB*, 153).

The form of "Asphodel," the triadic line, is the same as that
of "The Descent," the first poem in which Williams used the
technique. All the poems of *Journey to Love* and *The Desert Music* that use this form have in them something of the theme of
descent into memory. The triadic line forms a picture on the
page—the lines seem to cascade downward on the page in
waves, in falls. The picture presented on the page by the lines
shows the reader that descent is inevitable; the movement is
"downward to darkness, on extended wings," even in the
most beautiful lines.[17]

But the line gives the poet time and a steady voice to speak
against the fall into death, as a person has time to create beauty
in the measure of his or her life. The regularity of the three-
ply line has its advantages, for the lines are ordered and inevitable, too. Every fourth line will begin again at the margin of
the page. Williams sought out a sense of formal predictability
in his late poems; it was the lack of "inevitability" in Olson's
lines that led Williams to have some qualms over Olson's
verse.[18] The reader knows what to expect in terms of the formal progression of "Asphodel," and this leads to a certain
calm for poet and reader. Words ride the lines like ships. Williams' admiration for *The Iliad* permeates "Asphodel"; his
measure was his way of establishing a "sea-change," a sea-
beat, to match the roll of the ancient music (*IWWP*, 83). As
another aging poet reflected, "There was an ease of mind that
was like being alone in a boat at sea."[19]

But the poem does not merely roll and flow. When the poet

17. Stevens, *Poems*, 10.
18. "Letter to Cid Corman," dated May 16, 1983, HRHRC.
19. Stevens, *Poems*, 161.

speaks of the imagination's resistance against death, we can feel the tension of creation against destruction in the lines, the poet's defiance.

> Only the imagination is real!
>   I have declared it
>   time without end.
>   If a man die
>   it is because death
>   has first
>   possessed his imagination. (*PB*, 179)

The poet sets his words in the lines against the weather of death, much as he admired the starling's "manoeuvre" against the wind.

> I saw the two starlings
> coming in toward the wires.
> But at the last,
> just before the alighting, they
>
> turned in the air together
> and landed backwards!
> that's what got me—to
> face into the wind's teeth. (*CLP*, 88)

A tone and theme of simplicity permeates, penetrates the poems in *Pictures from Brueghel*. Williams liked the words "penetrate," "penetrant." As he stated in "The Descent of Winter" (1923), "Such must be the future: penetrant and simple—minus the scaffolding of the academic, which is a 'lie' in that it is inessential to the purpose as to the design" (*I*, 259). Particulars must suffice. At the end of "Asphodel" Williams sings,

> but an odor
>   as from our wedding
>   has revived for me
> and begun again to penetrate
>   into all crevices
>   of my world. (*PB*, 182)

The particular, the tangible thing seen or remembered, has the power to extend itself into the crevices of one's feeling and understanding, to create a world. The particular, the memory of a flower seen in boyhood, can transport the poet to the depths of the sea, to a sense of universality, or can show him the glint of light on the waves, the beauty of surfaces and order, of pageantry.

The simplicity in *Pictures from Brueghel* is the wise simplicity of an old man, one who is handing on what he knows to others, penetrating the future.

In the poem "Paul" Williams teaches his grandson how to fish.

> when you shall arrive
> as deep
> as you will need go
>
> to catch the blackfish
> the hook
> has been featly baited
>
> by the art you have
> and
> you do catch them (*PB*, 22)

Implicitly, unobtrusively, Williams is talking about style in this poem, rejoicing in his own style. Go deep, he advises his grandson, invent a strategy, a craft, to hook the fish or the reader. Translate that "glistening body," that sensual reality, into a language as bare and clean as the art of cutting can make the object. Enjoy the poem, share and revel in your style of cutting, in the way you make your line breaks, "however you / divide / and share." Surely the form of this poem is as clean and bare as possible, a fish cleanly gutted, or a line dropped to bait the reader.

The "scrupulous bareness"[20] of Williams' early poems becomes all the more stringent in the late poems. The discipline of careful word choice, "chastity" of speech, served the poet well in the poems composed in the triadic line as well as in the short poems. The triadic lines are like wires, humming.

All of the poems in *The Desert Music* and *Journey to Love* that are written in the triadic line seem to be part of one composition. The lines of the poems resemble chords and remind one

20. Miller, *Poets of Reality*, 344.

of the way music might be scored. The poems written in the new measure are part of the "fugal music" of Williams' personal epic, his journey through memory to renewal.

Poems from *Pictures from Brueghel*, written in short, terse lines, in triadic stanzas often, form a continuity with the other poems as well. For all the poems in the book have the bareness of language mentioned earlier, and all have common themes: simplicity, memory, renewal through art and love. The last books mark a turning point in Williams' writing, for in "Shadows" the poet says that "Memory / is liver than sight" (*PB*, 150). But Williams has been trained to see clearly all his life, and even what he sees in memory has a tangible clarity to it, like the image of Flossie at the altar.

The theme of simplicity is mentioned explicitly in several poems in the last books. In "The Host," where Williams describes nuns and a cleric in a restaurant, Williams says of what he sees and imagines, "It was a simple story" (*PB*, 94). In the poem "The Mental Hospital Garden" Williams talks of Saint Francis and says,

> All mankind
> grew to be his debtors,
> a simple story. (*PB*, 97)

The "simple story" is that "Love is in season." A mood of love, a season for a common language of love, permeates the one continuous "simple story" found in the late poems.

There is no mention of simplicity in "The Sparrow," but the poem is a statement about Williams' poetic style and mastery. Late in life the poet identifies his craft almost completely with his image of the sparrow.

> This sparrow
> who comes to sit at my window
> is a poetic truth
> more than a natural one. (*PB*, 129)

The sparrow is somewhat comic,

> Nothing even remotely
> subtle
> about his lovemaking.

But his technique is sharp.

> The way he swipes his bill
> across a plank
> to clean it,
> is decisive. (*PB*, 131)

Williams might be describing his own technique of cleaning up and shaping his lines. At the end the sparrow is no more than a "dried wafer," but the bird is more eloquent than ever in this state; he is a victim without bitterness,

> an effigy of a sparrow
> a dried wafer only,
> left to say
> and it says it
> without offense,
> beautifully;
> This was I,
> a sparrow.
> I did my best;
> farewell. (*PB*, 132)

Williams dedicates this poem to his father, who had died in 1918. The poem is Williams' justification of his work, his answer to a dream of his father returning from the dead to say, "severely, 'You know all that poetry you're writing. Well, it's no good'" (*A*, 14). After a lifetime Williams responds by becoming one with his images.

All of these parts of "a simple story" form a prelude to "Asphodel." Yet there is no mention of the word "simple" in that poem. In two rough-draft versions of "Asphodel" Williams refers to Asphodel as "a simple flower" (YALC) but deletes the comment in the final version. Perhaps Williams saw the comment as a note of explanation to himself that was unnecessary for the reader. Or he might have realized that asphodel, found in Homer's Hades, could not be as simple as all that.

The theme of simplicity is not mentioned in "Asphodel" because the poem demonstrates simplicity through the nature of its language without any need of self-conscious references. Words are things for Williams; he uses mostly simple words in the poem. The words used are the theme, the thing itself. "—Say it, no ideas but in things—" (*P*, 14).

In particulars, in single images, Williams sees the general, or universal. There are a "thousand topics / in an apple blossom," a generosity waiting to be explored in any single image; there are many women in Flossie, perhaps "a field made up of women / all silver-white" (*PB*, 160). (Though Williams thought he saw "endless wealth" in the arms of Flossie, we cannot help but remember that he still needed to play that "silver-white" field.)

Williams' imagery in "Asphodel" belongs to the magic world of the imagination where one image can be transformed into another, into its opposite even; metamorphosis does not frighten the imagination at play. The sea, the universal, becomes a garden, the ordered image, and then the image breaks open again, to release the sea as Williams sings,

> The whole world
>   became my garden!
> But the sea
>   which no one tends
>   is also a garden
>   when the sun strikes it
>   and the waves
>   are wakened. (*PB*, 156)

The sea, "that profound depth," casts up its treasures, its particulars.

> . . . there are the starfish
>   stiffened by the sun
>   and other sea wrack
>   and weeds. (*PB*, 156)

In an earlier poem, "Flowers by the Sea," Williams had shown the power of the imagination to create new, mythical forms with its "esemplastic" waves.[21] The imagination for Williams has the power to unbind, to loose the general from the

21. Samuel Taylor Coleridge, *Coleridge: Poetry and Prose* (New York, 1965), 173.

particular, and then to bring back the flow into an image of order.

> When over the flowery, sharp pasture's
> edge, unseen, the salt ocean
>
> lifts its form—chicory and daisies
> tied, released, seem hardly flowers alone
>
> but color and the movement—or the shape
> perhaps—of restlessness, whereas
>
> the sea is circled and sways
> peacefully upon its plantlike stem (*CEP*, 87)

Williams' imagination creates equivalents throughout "Asphodel," bringing diverse images into a unity through love.

> Are facts not flowers
> and flowers facts
> or poems flowers
> or all works of the imagination,
> interchangeable?
> Which proves
> that love
> rules them all. . . . (*PB*, 178)

Not only images, but the energy behind the images is one: "Light / the imagination / and love, / . . . maintain / all of a piece / their dominance" (*PB*, 180).

Williams' delight in contradictions, his embracing of transformations, reminds us of the tribal imagination as it describes its existence in "Magic Words (after Nalungiaq)," an Eskimo song.

> In the very earliest time,
> when both people and animals lived on earth,
> a person could become an animal if he wanted to
> and an animal could become a human being .
> . . . .
> All spoke the same language.
> That was the time when words were like magic.
> The human mind had mysterious powers.
> A word spoken by chance
> might have strange consequences.

It would suddenly come alive
and what people wanted to happen could happen—
all you had to do was say it.[22]

The form of "Asphodel," the triadic stanza in which three
lines form one unit, gives us a picture through structure of
how the one can contain many experiences and the many be
embraced as one. Often, the fourth line, or the opening line
of a new triadic unit, breaks the order just established, or
provides a counterpoint. With the line "But the sea," unity
surges into multiplicity again, proliferates itself.

A thousand topics
    in an apple blossom.
        The generous earth itself
gave us lief.
    The whole world
        became my garden!
But the sea
    which no one tends. . . . (*PB*, 155–56)

Williams admired Dante's use of the terza rima form, his
emphasis on structure. According to Williams, every four
lines of Dante's verse "contain a dissonance. . . . Throughout
the *Commedia* this fourth unrhymed factor, unobserved, is the
entrance of Pan to the Trinity which restores it to the candid
embrace of love . . ." (*SE*, 207). Williams' fourth line, "But the
sea," may be seen as an example of how Williams includes a
dissonance into his ordered world, how he floods the garden
with the chaotic depths of his love. In the fourth line "But" is
the loophole, the unfinished or broken-off place like that left
by the Hopi basket weaver who has to guard against a finished work. For if the design is finished, the weaver or the
poet is finished. And "Death / is not the end of it"; the spirits
must be allowed to enter. "Asphodel" ends with crevices, per-
meated with the odor of newly awakened love.

22. English workings by Edward Field, in Jerome Rothenberg (ed.), *Shaking the Pumpkin: Traditional Poetry of the Indian North Americas* (New York, 1972), 45. See also *Eskimo Songs and Stories*, trans. Edward Field (New York, 1973).

CHAPTER FOUR

The Measure of "Asphodel"

The typographic design of "Asphodel," the visual statement the poem makes, transmits a story in itself. The triadic lines stand out against the space of the page to remind us of the power of words to turn the void to account, emphasizing the dignity of speech against blankness. We have already signaled other messages or pictures that the poem's shape transmits: the waves and falls of lines across the page tell us that we are involved with the poet in a "sea-change," in a song that is guided by the poet's affinity with the water element, with feelings and the flow of memories. The sea always makes Williams think of *The Iliad*, and the poet's admiration for Homer's music sings out in every phrase or wave of "Asphodel." The poem's resemblance to a musical score adds more music to these waters.

"But all this doesn't get us far enough," Cid Corman writes to Williams, in one of his letters "On Measure" (October 9, 1953). Corman elaborates on what he sees as Williams' purpose in emphasizing the variable foot and triadic line.

It is a beginning or a way of beginning. Your search for measure, for a particular elucidation, springs, at least partly I'm inclined to think, from a desire to found the long poem or more accurately the "extended" poem, on a sound continuing ground swell. In a way, we're back at the epic again, or the tragedy. Extended form. And this demands a coherence that is hard, if not impossible, to fulfill through lyrical intentions. Intonations. You said it yourself, when we spoke of it: the problem is to discover a modus for the extended poem, to prove a modus in the extended practise.[1]

Williams had not yet published the whole of "Asphodel" when Cid Corman wrote this letter. But Corman was right. The measure that Williams had been seeking provided the lines and their breaks, the continuity that he could put into practice in the extended poem "Asphodel." Each line or segment lends itself to the movement of the whole poem, furthering the action or swell of the piece.

Corman's reference to the epic and to tragedy, to the "sound continuing ground swell" required for the long poem, sends us back to Williams' early statement, "Speech Rhythm" (1913). There Williams outlines an idea of action that he wants his poems to embody.

No action, no creative action is complete but a period from a greater action going in rhythmic course, i.e., an Odyssey, is rightly considered not an isolated unit but a wave of a series from hollow through crest to hollow. No part in its excellence but partakes of the essential nature of the whole.
This is the conception of the action I want.
In the other direction, inward: Imagination creates an image, point by point, piece by piece, segment by segment—into a whole, living. But each part as it plays into its neighbor, each segment into its neighbor segment and every part into every other, causing the whole— exists naturally in rhythm, and as there are waves there are tides and as there are ridges in the sand there are bars after bars. . . .[2]

Behind the poem, before its existence, Williams holds a concept of action that is heard and transmitted, not through words but through rhythm: "The rhythm itself is a thing apart and no sound. Upon this the wordy passions string sounds as they strain toward the perfect image."[3] The poet begins by listening, searching deep into his life or into the life of things; as Henri Bergson explained: "And so, by a kind of intellectual

1. Cid Corman, "Letters on Measure," *Origin*, III (April, 1966), 17.
2. See Mike Weaver's *William Carlos Williams: The American Background* (Cambridge, England, 1971), 82–83, for Williams' full statement entitled "Speech Rhythm."
3. *Ibid.*, 83.

auscultation, to feel the throbbings of its soul," the poet intuits the rhythm his poem requires.[4] Words enter later, in the way characters enter a play to further the action. Though Williams the aging poet confided to Corman that his sense of measure was largely intuitive, defined by his ear, Corman rejected the distinction between thought and intuition.

My assault is on the "double", on the abstracting insistence, where "instinct" is put here and "thought" there. In a very real sense thinking is an instinct. But more important here, I believe, is that art is precisely the point where the interplay of mind and instinct (or blood, if you want to stick with DHL) offers life its richest interpretation, penetration, in form, informed, which means as myth, as Lekakis, who so well knows the measure of sculpture, has said is "preparation for death". (And I think of Malinowski here too.)[5]

The action of Williams' late poetry, all of that verse written in the triadic line, but especially "Asphodel," might be defined as a "preparation for death," or a meditation on death's approach, though the poetry is a celebration of life and in no way morbid. The concept of action that is being applied here is a profound and unifying one, not at all mechanical, extending itself beyond the poem's design but giving design a reason. The unifying action that underlies the words and movements of "Asphodel" provides us with another way of understanding the poem's depths.

It was, of course, Aristotle who brought the concept of action in drama and in verse to readers' attention. In the *Poetics* Aristotle tells us that tragedy imitates a serious and complete action, "and of a certain magnitude." The lyric poet, too, the "maker," imitates action. Aristotle uses *The Odyssey* and *The Iliad* to illustrate his interest in poems that in their greatness have an action that is one, single.[6]

Francis Fergusson, in his introduction to Aristotle's *Poetics* and in *The Idea of the Theatre*, has helped modern readers to understand the meaning of "action": as what Dante called

4. Henri Bergson, *An Introduction to Metaphysics* (New York, 1912), 36.
5. Corman, "Letters on Measure," 16.
6. *Aristotle's Poetics*, with an introductory essay by Francis Fergusson, trans. S. H. Butcher (New York, 1961), 61, 67.

a "movement-of-spirit," a unifying movement of the psyche or a motivation that precedes the play or poem. Characters, words, follow the action. Francis Fergusson reminds us that not only tragedy but great lyric poetry also has its action or movement-of-spirit, and he quotes Coleridge on this point: "'The unity of action . . . is not properly a rule, but in itself the great end, not only of drama, but of the lyric, epic, even to the candle-flame of the epigram—not only of poetry, but of poesy in general, as the proper generic term inclusive of all the fine arts as its species.'"[7]

The action of "Asphodel" is not just "poiesis," or the making of the poem, though surely the poet's concentration on craft and on the theme of making (or losing) poetry is one of the poem's central concerns. The action is one of spiritual renewal through memory, a renewal of love through the poem's "journey to love." With this concept of action in mind, the action of the poet's listening to the rhythm of his memories, we should not be disturbed to learn that "Asphodel" was entitled "The River of Heaven" early on its conception and may first have been inspired by Ginsberg's verses rather than by Flossie's attentions.[8] The measure, the poem's rhythm, came first, and the story ensued as it had to, as Williams' illnesses led him closer to Flossie and her protection than ever before.

What is the action of "Asphodel"? The rhythm of the poem

7. Francis Fergusson, "Introduction," *Aristotle's Poetics*, 2–44; Fergusson, *The Idea of a Theater* (1949; rpr. Garden City, 1953), particularly 206–255. Fergusson's comments on Aristotle's 'apperceptive intelligence' (254) remind us of how Williams listened for the new "measure" before he knew specifically what he was looking for: "The objections of the semanticists to Aristotle's epistemology with its basis in the *nous*, or 'apperceptive intelligence' . . . represent an important and stubborn contemporary habit of mind. Aristotle is not as *inaverti* as they think; 'what he has that they haven't got' is not naïve credulity but a recognition that we are aware of things and people 'before predication,' as he puts it. The histrionic sensibility, the perception of action, is such a primitive and direct awareness." Fergusson quotes Coleridge's essay on Othello on pp. 9–10 of his "Introduction" to *Aristotle's Poetics*.

8. See Williams' unpublished notes for "Asphodel," YALC. Also, see Paul Mariani's article "Paterson 5: The Whore/Virgin and the Wounded One-Horned Beast," for Ginsberg's influence on "Asphodel" in its early stages. *Denver Quarterly*, XIII (Summer, 1978), 102–129.

is staccato; there is a flow and an impediment to the flow. The action of the poem is twofold, as is appropriate for the action of a love poem, one in which two people are deeply concerned. The primary action of "Asphodel" is "to get through the darkness with song" (and, to move toward the beloved), the same basic action that we may discern in Dante's *Commedia* and in earlier great Orphic myths. The secondary action, that resists movement rather than encourages it, is "to hold off time and death with poetry." At some point in the poem, perhaps where the lines break and then renew themselves, these actions of moving forward and holding back combine. The bones or phrases of the poem that might want to stick in the throat ease and dissolve to become one with the sea's flow. Williams likens himself, or the bard in the poem,

> to a blind old man
> whose bones
> have the movement
> of the sea,
> a sexless old man
> for whom it is a sea
> of which his verses
> are made up. (*PB*, 166)

The poem rises and falls in its waves of action, as well as surging forward and holding back. Williams speaks of the desirable quality of these motions in "Speech Rhythm." "The one thing essential to rhythm is not sound but motion, of the two kinds: forward and up and down, rapidity of motion and quality of motion. Thus the number of sounds in the rhythm unit do not because of their number give the unit any quality but only as they give motion in one of the two directions."[9] The phrases that "launch" "Asphodel" remind us not only of *The Aeneid* but of the opening surge of Pound's *Cantos*, where the rhythmic and thematic associations of Canto One to Chapter Ten in the *Odyssey* take us back to Odysseus' journey through hell. The ease and naturalness of Williams' opening

9. Quoted by Mike Weaver, *William Carlos Williams*, 83.

lines provide a marked contrast to the gusto, the muscular push of Pound's opening lines, which carry with them an Anglo-Saxon linguistic sensibility.

> And then went down to the ship,
> Set keel to breakers, forth on the godly sea, and
> We set up mast and sail on that swart ship.[10]

Williams' music is more gentle, yet the poem still voyages. The direct statement that closes the first sentence of "Asphodel" ("I come, my sweet, / to sing to you") helps to further the forward motion of the poem. And throughout "Asphodel" the references to *The Iliad* and to the "catalogue of ships" remind us that words ride the waves of lines forward to the rhythm, the literary rhythm, of the sea. (Though lists, "catalogues," may be thought of as vertical.)

There is a vertical design to "Asphodel," a depth charge that is evident not only in the mythic theme but in the design of the poem, and later, as we shall see, in the rhythm. We can see the rise and fall of the triadic line, as each third line descends to a fourth, or a new opening stanza. The overall picture may be one of a descent, but the song creates an upward movement-of-spirit, toward light, contemplation, "theoria," where the motive is "'to grasp and understand' some truth."[11] The "steps" of the poem may be climbed upward. As Williams says to Flossie,

> Let me, for I know
> you take it hard,
> with good reason,
> give the steps
> if it may be
> by which you shall mount,
> again to think well
> of me. (*PB*, 171)

If we are to consider carefully Williams' idea that the number of syllables in a phrase may be important in the way that they further the poem's movement (both forward and rising

10. Ezra Pound, *The Cantos* (New York, 1956), 3.
11. Fergusson, "Introduction" to *Aristotle's Poetics*, 10.

and falling), then passages like the following may tell us something about the poem's swell:

> I have learned much in my life
>   from books
>   and out of them
>   about love.
>   Death
>   is not the end of it. *(PB,* 157)

If each phrase or foot gets a steady and fairly consistent beat, then "death" gets more time in this passage than the other phrases; "about love" is close in terms of how much stress time the word "love" will get. (A half-beat must be allowed for "about.") "Death," the single syllable, gives us the falling motion; this fall comes off of the edge of "about love" (a steadying phrase, possibly seen-heard as a slightly rising motion). The pause between "Death" and the rest of the sentence ironically furthers the action. Because the sentence has been split, we await its end, but the poet is telling us that the end will come in his own time. Through the steady but staccato tempo, the poet controls the idea of death's approach and effect.

"Is not the end of it," the phrase containing more syllables than other feet in the passage, resolves the issue, both in theme (Williams makes a firm statement) and in tone. The effect of a series of monosyllabic words is firmness; the phrase is steadying and carries with it the sense of rising motion. The phrase both stops "death" and tells us that there will be more music and more love. The poem does not always work this way: sometimes lines with the fewest syllables get the upward stress; the longer phrases seem to be understated.

> Love
>   to which you too shall bow
>   along with me—
>   a flower
>   a weakest flower
>   shall be our trust. . . . *(PB,* 161)

"Love," the single syllable, carries equal weight and impact with "shall be our trust" and compresses the thought. Clearly

Williams worked with and against a system of using extra sounds for the rising and falling motions. Some words get more weight because they get more time and have more of a message to carry. "Love" and "shall be our trust" have a firm and steadying effect, a flatness that is reassuring after the reference to bowing and weakness.

Williams' own reading of Book I of "Asphodel," recorded at the University of Puerto Rico in April, 1954 (and on tape at the Rutherford Public Library), gives us more clues as to how the measure of the poem actually works, at least in one performance.[12] Williams' reading on this tape is only one possible reading of "Asphodel." He read his own poems with some variations at each reading—we can discern a difference in his delivery of the triadic line on the Caedmon recording (taped at the Williams' home in June, 1954) from the Puerto Rico recording of triadic lines.[13] Other readers besides Williams will also have different and valid interpretations of the sound of his poem. The emphasis on the reader's role in interpreting the oral music, the flexibility the reader has in performance through Williams' nontraditional score, does not make the structural quality of the poem any less sound (as critics of Williams' ideas on the variable foot are eager to say, that the "system" is too imprecise to be a guide for reading). Any poem, even one written in the most traditional meter, will be read differently by different readers.

That there are inconsistencies in Williams' reading has also to do with his state of health. His speech impediments after his strokes made it hard for him to read with steadiness and vigor at times. But these impediments do not prevent the music from coming through, as Robert Lowell reminds us in his description of Williams' moving performance of "Asphodel" at Wellesley: "The poet appeared, one whole side partly paralyzed, his voice just audible, and here and there a word mis-

12. William Carlos Williams, "Asphodel, That Greeny Flower, Book I," recorded in April, 1954, at the University of Puerto Rico. Tape at the Rutherford Free Public Library.
13. William Carlos Williams, *William Carlos Williams Reads His Poetry* (1954).

read. No one stirred." "No one stirred," because Williams had "delivered [to his listeners] what was impossible"; Lowell goes on to describe the terrific impact on the audience of the poem that went "beyond poetry." The effect of the reading was a triumph for both the poet and the poem.[14]

Williams' voice on the tape of the Puerto Rico reading does not sound strong, but we can hear that he wants his listeners to be impressed with the poem's motion. The listener will note right away that Williams allows himself liberties with the basic tempo, and these liberties usually have to do with the passages that speak of time or motion. Williams speeds up to a kind of double-time when he reads this passage:

> But the sea
>   which no one tends
>   is also a garden
>   when the sun strikes it
>   and the waves
>   are wakened. (*PB*, 156)

The idea of the waves' wakening seems to have caught up Williams' voice and impelled his song. He also speeds up with

> It is like Homer's
>   catalogue of ships:
>   it fills up the time. (*PB*, 159)

"It fills up the time" is in triple-time. Through this hurrying Williams lets us know that boredom (perhaps his own boredom as an invalid at home) is oppressive, even as it can be a motivation to creativity.

The listener also notices that Williams does not always keep to his line breaks as he has marked them. For example, Williams reads "Listen while I talk on / against time" (*PB*, 154) as "Listen / while I talk on / against time." Perhaps these variations on the poem's score are the performer's prerogative, as a singer of oral poetry might have varied a traditional story a little with each telling. Denise Levertov, though, who is an ex-

14. Robert Lowell, "William Carlos Williams," in J. Hillis Miller (ed.), *William Carlos Williams: A Collection of Critical Essays* (Englewood Cliffs, 1966), 159.

tremely disciplined reader as well as writer, tried to convince Williams that he would have been better off to have read strictly in keeping with his scored lines. Levertov says that Williams had to agree.

> On his records he'd sometimes ignore a line break, and he'd pause in the middle of a line in other places because he didn't have full control over his speech by then; and I, being sassy, took him to task for not observing his own scores. I read to him his own poems according to the way I thought they were scored. And you have only my word for it, although maybe Flossie remembers and would back me up, but believe me he said, "You're absolutely right and if I were able to give public readings now that's the way I would do it."[15]

Williams' failure to keep to his scored lines does not mean that the score is not a good one; perhaps other poets and readers can do a better job with a reading of his poems than he did. Certainly, younger poets like Levertov understood and have furthered Williams' work.

We can learn more than a story about tempo and line breaks from Williams' taped reading at Puerto Rico if we know what to listen for. If each segment or foot of the poem furthers the action, then we must look to the stressed beat or inner life of each phrase to tell us more about the poem's movement-of-spirit. Williams has already instructed us in his letter to Eberhardt to place one beat per measure. Each line will have its own word or words with a primary stress (for that is how we speak), a word "central to the sky" or space "which ranges round it." Around the stressed word, other words in the line will gather like "a whole flood / of sister memories" to the flower's odor.

The Puerto Rico reading gives us clues as to a possible alignment of stressed beats within "Asphodel." In the first three lines of "Asphodel" the poem presents us with the image of "asphodel" and describes it for us. The action of presenting the image, the flower, is furthered by Williams' stressed reading of "asphodel," "buttercup," and "branching" within their

15. Denise Levertov, *Denise Levertov: In Her Own Province* (New York, 1979), 69.

respective lines. This string of primary beats gives us the oral clue that the image, the flower, is expanding; "buttercup" and "branching" connect musically not only by alliteration but by stress. "Greeny flower" and "stem" seem to get secondary but important stresses in the reading. The effect in this reading is an interplay of colors ("greeny" and "buttercup") reinforced by stresses; the secondary stress of "stem" stabilizes the third line. The poem has a root, a "stem," a stability within its swell, a vertical line of sounds and messages as well as a horizontal one. Although the stressed beats in the vertical pattern may not always have a syntactic connection, they do convey an impression in their overall effect of a vertical score within the forward-moving line, the effect of a blossoming flower on its stem.

It is hard to know whether to include the fourth line, "save that it's green and wooden," in the action of stanza one or two. Perhaps the line, the hesitation, "save that . . . ," with its pun on "save," is a link between the two stanzas or waves of action. "Green" and "wooden" both get primary stresses, carry equal weight. On the horizontal level, the way that we usually read the line across, we are being given the symbolic message and the musical message (through the repetition of "n" sounds) that both life and death are included in this image that expands into memory's song. (The visual message that we get is a connection between "save" and "green" because those monosyllabic words are of the same length.) "Save" gets a secondary stress in Williams' reading. The next primary stresses that the poet makes are on "come" and "sing." "You" is secondary in stress, though we might wish it were otherwise, to reinforce the poem's sentimental mood. The action in this stanza, as we hear it in Williams' reading, is "to come" (to approach the beloved), and "to sing," which is the action of the poem as a whole. This phrase is repeated again toward the end of Book I, without lines two, three and four, without description, with the action only, that is so moving in its directness.

The "green" and "wooden" flower that Williams brings to us and to Flossie calls to mind a statement that Williams made in a letter to R. Beum (1950): "No one has the guts to dream of a possible metric that will blossom out of the past as a flower blossoms out of a stick of wood."[16] Williams' love poem is always a poem about a commitment to a new metrics as well as to renewed love, though the reader never experiences the concern for craftsmanship as an intrusion. Craft is what carries Williams' love.

On the Caedmon recording, "William Carlos Williams Reading His Poems" (taped at his home in June), we can get a better sense of Williams' idea of his craft through his performance of his poetry than we are able to gather from the slightly earlier recording made in Puerto Rico. Williams read with a strong and steady voice in the Caedmon record, and he keeps up an even tempo. Perhaps he felt more comfortable recording at home than on tour and could do a better job in familiar surroundings. The meaning of Williams' idea of the variable foot becomes clear as one listens to the way he keeps up a beat that punctuates his speech rhythms. Though there are only twenty-one lines of "Work in Progress" (the last twenty-one lines of "Asphodel," Book I) on this recording, side one of the album contains Williams' reading of six poems from "The Desert Music and Other Poems" (1954), all written in the triadic line. From this recording we can hear what Williams was trying to accomplish in establishing a reliable but flexible measure. As Williams wrote to Beum, "The best thing you can say of me is that you *do* find me in smooth, rhythmical cadences."[17] The most sceptical listener cannot miss the regular cadences in Williams' recording for Caedmon.

When Williams reads "The Descent," the first poem he had written in the triadic line (from *Paterson*, Book II), we can hear in the smooth cadences certain stressed words to each line. These stresses tell a story in themselves and reinforce the poem's story. In the following stanzas I have marked the primary and secondary stresses as Williams reads them:

16. William Carlos Williams to R. Beum, January 5, 1950 (uncatalogued, UB).

17. *Ibid*.

```
        1        2
The descent beckons
                1        2
        as the ascent beckoned.
                    1        2
                Memory is a kind
            1
of accomplishment,
            2        1
        a sort of renewal
                1
            even
    1                2        2        2        2
an initiation, since the spaces it opens are new places. . . . (PB, 73)
```

Within the poet's forward movement, certain words align in a vertical pattern; we hear a line of impressions and understand through stress as well as through direct statement that "ascent," "descent," "memory," and "initiation" are interconnected. Through stress, vertical steps are created, further impressing upon us the poem's story: this poem will be a voyage inward, "down and out." This inner line of stresses reminds us of a passage from Denise Levertov's "A Tree Telling of Orpheus" that states the way in which the poem "descends a scale" even within its more direct story of a descent through hell. A tree, awakened by Orpheus, sings this passage:

And at the heart of my wood
(so close I was to becoming man or a god)
        there was a kind of silence, a kind of sickness,
            something akin to what men call boredom, something
(the poem descended a scale, a stream over stones)
            that gives to a candle a coldness
                in the midst of its burning, he said.[18]

In the background, as it were, of their reading of "Asphodel," those readers who have familiarized themselves with the poems in *Pictures from Brueghel* can still hear the music of "The Descent." The connection between the poems written in

18. Denise Levertov, "A Tree Telling of Orpheus," *Stony Brook*, I/II (Post-Fall, 1968), 21.

the triadic line is not just a visual or a thematic one but a musical one, a rhythm we remember having heard. This effect is stronger if one has the tendency to read poetry aloud, but probably the "background music" can still be heard by readers who just "listen" to what they are reading. There is a kind of implied polyphony in Williams' "fugal" music of the 1950s that ties the poems together, not merely by their design but by their rhythm, and that superimposes on "Asphodel" the music of a descent first experienced in *Paterson*. Lines that seem to be simple statements in "Asphodel" become more complex as they are enriched by our memories.

The triadic line with its stressed beats provides us with a mnemonic device. The reader who has scanned the poem in his or her own reading, or who has heard Williams' Caedmon recording, will remember sections of the long poems because of the regular cadences and the association of stresses that remain in memory. This mnemonic device, that Williams termed "the variable foot," helps the reader to remember verses in the way formulaic phrases and quantitative lines must have reminded the audience of what to listen for, or what to sing, in verses in the Greek oral tradition.

Whether we read "Asphodel" ourselves, or listen to Williams, we find that the sound effects of the poem are gentle, even though the poem's action includes a struggle against time and death. The music of the words has a falling-off effect; many lines end with unstressed beats (in words such as "flower," "buttercup," "wooden," "together"). In the first seven lines we find that at least four phrases end with secondary or tertiary stresses; the "er" sounds in particular give a falling-off effect. Even the lines that end on stressed beats are weak endings within Williams' system of stresses. In line three, "stem" ends one line with a stress, but not a strong one—Williams reads this line with the emphasis on "branching." The sound of the poem reminds us that the poem is a love poem,

> a love of nature, of people,
> animals,

> a love engendering
> gentleness and goodness
>   that moved me
>   and *that* I saw in you. (*PB*, 160)

Williams stresses the "you" strongly on the Puerto Rico tape; here he is speaking to Flossie. Though Williams protests that he is not "too feeble" to manage any other topic than "a weakest flower," we do seem to hear a kind of physical weakness at times in the poetry, calling to mind a passage from "The Descent."

> With evening, love wakens
>   though its shadows
>   which are alive by reason
> of the sun shining—
>   grow sleepy now and drop away
>   from desire . (*PB*, 73)

Even when Williams sings of his purpose, to defeat death with the imagination's powers ("Death / is not the end of it"), the sound effects do not compare in strength with other extended poems whose wave-like motions roll in defiance of decay. Compare Williams' use of vowel sounds with the long vowel sounds in Milton's "Lycidas" ("Flames in the forehead of the morning sky: / So Lycidas sunk low, but mounted high"); or Wordsworth's "The Prelude" ("The immeasurable height / Of woods decaying, never to be decayed").[19] Milton and Wordsworth pin the line's end firmly with the so-called "masculine ending" or stressed ending; the resonating vowel sounds insist on the triumph of the imagination over death. Williams will use long vowel sounds, but usually these are softened by short vowel sounds in the same phrases: "I come, my sweet, / to sing to you." At their strongest or highest pitch, Williams' sounds seem to stabilize a line rather than to raise its pitch in any dramatic way. Williams counts on timing and momentum to convey his drama.

19. John Milton, "Lycidas," in M. H. Abrams (ed.), *Norton Anthology of English Literature* (2 vols.; New York, 1962), I, 889; William Wordsworth, "The Prelude," *Norton Anthology of English Literature*, II, 154.

>   The light
>   for all time shall outspeed
>   the thunder crack. (*PB*, 181)

The sounds of "Asphodel" are gentler than those of the passages noted from Wordsworth or Milton, because Williams is writing a love poem in his old age (he has a lot to make up for to Flossie, and had best "make peace," approach softly). But also, I think, there is another reason for the softer sound effects in Williams' poetry than in the other poems cited. Although Williams believes in the powers of the imagination, our age is not one that supports the idea of the immortality of spirit, art, or mind. Milton had religion to support his long "a" sounds; Wordsworth had nature. Williams has only his love, and his song. Yet the mythic, eternal dimension of the poetry continues to resonate in the movement, the gestures that take the poet through hell in pursuit of his love.

Part III

THE DESCENT

CHAPTER FIVE

The Descent Beckons

The theme of descent is explicit, central to the language of Williams' early work, *Kora in Hell* (1920). "Down, down. The whole family take shovels, babies and all! Down, down! Here's Tenochtitlan!" (*K*, 40). The language is violent, spasmodic, as if Williams is exploiting the nervous "pace of speech" typical of his early writings. As Williams explained to Edith Heal, "The rhythmic pace was the pace of speech, an excited pace because I was excited when I wrote. I was discovering . . ." (*IWWP*, 15). The persona of the character who wants his family to pick up shovels sounds half-mad for the earth. He speaks of digging as important enough to be a collective enterprise. What sounds like grave digging turns out to be archeology, excavation, discovery of hidden cities and treasures in what had appeared to be dirt and chaos.

"What is below is like that which is above"[1] for Williams—the magic of opposites is at work in Williams' poetry of descent: "Burrow, burrow, burrow! There's sky that way too if the pit's deep enough—so the stars tell us" (*K*, 16). Here is a voice Blake might have cheered, a voice agreeing with the dictum that "Without Contraries is no progression." In "Thel's Motto" Blake had asked, "Does the Eagle know what is in the

---

1. John Senior, *The Way Down and Out: The Occult in Symbolist Literature* (New York, 1968), 28.

pit? / Or wilt thou go ask the Mole?"[2] The mole becomes an eagle if it burrows long enough. The world is turned around through the imagination. As Williams says, "There is neither beginning nor end to the imagination but it delights in its own seasons reversing the usual order at will" (*K*, 15). Behind the burrowing there is a yearning for fresh air, a hope for ascendance: "Often when the descent seems well marked there will be a subtle ascent over-ruling it so that in the end when the degradation is fully anticipated the person will be found to have emerged upon a hilltop" (*K*, 47).

A persona in *Kora* who sounds like Williams expresses the poet's hope that there may be a point to all this digging; the experience of plunging into a chaos of experimentation in language and in life may lead to a recovery of creative power: "One never knows—perhaps we'll bring back Euridice—this time!" (*K*, 11). Kora and Euridice are seen as one, the buried or darkened side of the poet's imaginative life; Kora also represents the difficulties Williams was experiencing in his marriage, a lack of communication that turned him toward poetry.

The quest in *Kora* is the poet's work to rescue his strength through the exploratory powers of language. Williams admitted, "I thought of myself as being under the earth, buried in other words, but as any plant is buried, retaining the power to come again." The descent is a working to free the buried self, through voices in *Kora*, or through imagery in the later poems. Williams rarely indulges in personal introspection or self-pity in his poetry. "I have always believed in keeping myself out of the picture. When I spoke of flowers, I *was* a flower, with all the prerogatives of flowers, especially the right to come alive in the Spring" (*IWWP*, 21).

In *Kora* Williams identified with the figure of Kora. "It was Persephone gone into Hades, into hell. Kora was the springtime of the year; my year, my self was being slaughtered. What was the use of denying it? For relief, to keep myself from planning and thinking at all, I began to write in earnest"

2. William Blake, *The Portable Blake* (New York, 1965), 250, 279.

(*A*, 158). Williams' book *Kora in Hell*, a work he liked particularly well, was the odd flower that grew from his deliberate struggle with a sense of artistic barrenness. Later in "Asphodel," he says,

> I was cheered
>   when I came first to know
>   that there were flowers also
>   in hell. (*PB*, 153)

Williams' first mention of "asphodel" in his writings occurs in *Kora*. "Asphodel" is depicted as a pure flower, an image gleaned from suffering, "cleaner fare" than most of the corrupt society knows. But asphodel is ominous; as the poet bends over it he says, "I will lead you to fields you know nothing of" (*K*, 32), referring to the fields of the dead found in Homer's *Odyssey*, and to the "fields" opened by the imagination.

In the myth of Kore or Persephone, the Maiden is lured to a field of flowers before she is ravished.[3] Seeking wholeness, the poet assumes in his work all the roles from the archiac drama or ritual of Kore. By his own account Williams is the victim, but he is also the seducer, fantasizing as he imagines the rape of "Beautiful Thing" in *Paterson*; leading the reader out toward the "fields" of his prose poem in *Kora*. He is the rescuer, Hermes or Dionysus, the poet who restores the Maiden to her mother; by his art he restores his own lost self or voice to the world. In some versions of the myth Hermes leads Persephone to a marriage with the "bearded god" of the underworld.[4] "Asphodel" completes a story begun in *Kora*. "By my father's beard," Williams says in "Asphodel," and that phrase propels the poem toward the depths of Williams' contemplation of death, toward Kore-Demeter (Flossie watering her plants), and toward a final image of marriage.

In *Kora*, a poem about wounds, Williams has not found a

---

3. C. Kerényi, *Eleusis: Archetypal Image of Mother and Daughter* (New York, 1977), 34. "It was a dangerous region to which Kore let herself be lured in search for flowers . . . ," 35.

4. *Ibid.*, 173.

cure for the slights he has suffered at the world's hands. He has a difficult time assuming the voice of Demeter, the nurturer, though the expression of his pain in song is by its nature a consolation. In "Asphodel," however, where Williams is finally able to sing in the triadic line, to reach out to Flossie, he is able to take on or take in her role. He can "water his roots" with an "all-night rain of music,"[5] restore himself and Flossie.

The Kore-Persephone and the Euridice myths, variations on the theme of descent and rescue of the female creative principle, concerned Williams throughout his life. When Williams refers to Persephone in his poetry he relies on the reader's knowledge of basic aspects of the myth, not the more esoteric aspects of the mysteries.

Yet it is tempting to read the secrets of an initiatory ritual into "Asphodel"—even if the more esoteric parallels are only unconsciously alive there—to see in the "greeny" but "wooden" flower the ancient vegetation goddesses Rhea, Kore, Demeter, Persephone. It is tempting to see Persephone, the hidden one, the spiritual mystery of rebirth, in the cave drawings Williams reminds us of, and to see her veiled in the marriage ceremony. But such secrets, if they are in the poem, lie deeply embedded in its more obvious and deliberate mythic pattern.

Williams drives deep in his poetry as a result of his yearning to see. Inevitably, his curiosity leads him to examine the depths of a situation, even an explosive, emotionally dangerous situation.

There is beauty in the bellow of the BLAST . . . —To me beauty is purity. To me it is discovery . . .
And for this you are willing to smash—
Yes, everything.—To go down into hell. —Well let's look. (*I*, 171)

We may assume that Williams did not deliberately seek out suffering but had it in his nature to follow his feelings and to

5. Denise Levertov, "A Tree Telling of Orpheus," *Stony Brook* I/II (Post-Fall, 1968), 23.

look at them honestly. As he says to Flossie in "Asphodel,"
often he "found himself" in difficulty.

> I cannot say
> > that I have gone to hell
> > > for your love
> but often
> > found myself there
> > > in your pursuit. (*PB*, 156)

As the lines move downward on the page, speaking of Williams' journies to hell, they signal to us that this poem will
make an inner journey. By repetition, Williams etches a memory, a picture of depths. The poem has several ways of achiev-
ing its journey to emotional depths. "Asphodel" is reflexive,
referring to Williams' life and literary life in a way that adds
resonances to his images. The image of "Asphodel," found in
Kora, reminds us of the poet's early struggle and early work,
of the connection between "asphodel" and the underworld in
myth and art, of the continuity of dreams and the unconscious. Williams tells us in "Asphodel" about how he pressed
flowers into his book as a boy, "The asphodel, / forebodingly, /
among them." He brings us "reawakened, / a memory of
those flowers" (*PB*, 155), a memory of his boyhood, and of the
Autobiography, where he speaks of gathering asphodel while
at school in Switzerland (*A*, 29). "Any poem that has worth
expresses the whole life of the poet," Williams says in *Paterson*
(261). But some poems are more densely packed with life than
others; perhaps more than any of his other poems "Asphodel" sings to us of what Williams has lived and written.

This personal mythology, recall of meaningful images and
"spots of time," adds depth to the poem, as do the folkloric
and mythic elements. The contest between light and darkness
in "Asphodel" is an agon found in fairy tales and folklore.
Persecution is old, Williams reminds us, with his references
to the witchcraft trials. The bomb threatens us with darkness,
while the poets, explorers and great men of culture move
through the lines of "Asphodel" with their "palms going / al-

ways to the light." The outcome is by no means certain, though in the "Coda" Williams asserts that "The light / for all time shall outspeed / the thunder crack."

We can also interpret the "Coda" in the light of an older drama. The Hierophant at Eleusis, home of Persephone's mysteries, beat an "echeion," an "instrument with the voice of thunder." The thunder signaled the opening of the underworld, heralded a vision of death. The torchlights that followed thunder were a sign of revelation and rebirth in the midst of this meeting with death.[6] Williams reverses the order of the archaic ceremony, "light takes precedence," as the poem celebrates a mystery of awakening and reunion.

"Asphodel" contains in its structure the archetypal pattern of descent and return, death and rebirth. This initiatory pattern is of primary concern, since Williams continued to write about the seeing derived from struggle, from "descent," all of his life. Williams' first long poem, "The Wanderer" (*CEP*, 3), tells of his initiation as a poet and seer. The poet is led by a magical old hag through Paterson and the surrounding landscape, and is immersed in the "filthy Passaic" river as a baptism. The river enters the poet, taking·him back to origins, and then takes him down to the depths of himself.

> Then the river began to enter my heart,
> Eddying back cool and limpid
> Into the crystal beginning of its days.
> But with the rebound it leaped forward:
> Muddy, then black and shrunken
> Till I felt the utter depth of its rottenness
> The vile breadth of its degradation
> And dropped down knowing this was me now. (*CEP*, 11)

The downward motion corresponds to a movement into older memories, then turns to an ascent and a new beginning. Finally, time is transcended through the poet's identification with motion, through the fluidity of the imagination.

6. Kerényi, *Eleusis*, 84.

But she lifted me and the water took a new tide
Again into the older experiences,
And so, backward and forward,
It tortured itself within me
Until time had been washed finally under,
And the river had found its level
And its last motion had ceased
And I knew all—it became me. (*CEP*, 11–12)

Time stretches back and forth on these lines, inside the poet, carrying him to a past beyond his personal experience, much as the lines weave Rilke into a vision in "The Third Elegy."

. . . How he gave himself up to it! Loved.
Loved his interior world, his interior jungle,
that primal forest within, on whose mute overthrownness,
green-lit, his heart stood. Loved. Left it, continued
into his own roots and out into violent beginning
where his tiny birth was already outlived. Descended,
lovingly, into the older blood, the ravines
where Frightfulness lurked, still gorged with the fathers.[7]

Williams and Rilke go deep in these visionary poems, charged with the task of seeing. The poets live what the occultists believe, that self-realization is the great task, that it is "progressive discovery of the layers of the psyche which is not mere ego" but includes universal substance. "All things live according to pulse, or breath, or rhythm," which the poet enters and shares in the lines of his verse. In the cycles of birth and decay shared by all things, "in the cycles, both collectively in history and individually in men, all souls must eventually be all things. The task of individual man as we know him, of the times as we live in them, is to leave things as they seem in order to discover the unknown, which is often symbolized as a descent into Hell."[8] In "Asphodel" the poet's lines weave a picture of his memories in an attempt to "discover the

7. Rainer Maria Rilke, *Duino Elegies*, trans. J. B. Leishman and Stephen Spender (New York, 1963), 37–39.
8. Senior, *The Way Down and Out*, 40–41.

unknown," to look at the hell of approaching death and try to ward it off with song. We are left with the tapestry of a wedding woven in light; the ceremonial flower has a "moral odor" that transcends time's destructiveness.

The theme of descent and ascent returns in "Asphodel"— "The Wanderer" and "Asphodel" form a circle. The beginning and ending of Williams' writings interconnect with their stories of endings and new beginnings.

> The (self) direction has been changed
> the serpent
> its tail in its mouth
> "the river has returned to its beginnings"
> and backward
> (and forward). . . . (*P*, 271)

Williams quotes lines from "The Wanderer" in *Paterson V*, but he syncopates them now; words are loosened in the waves of lines and allowed to flow. Again he sings of the mysterious river that "tortures itself" within him before he can become one with his vision:

> it tortures itself within me
> until time has been finally washed under:
> and "I knew all (or enough)
> it became me . " (*P*, 271)

The river flows toward itself, toward an "impalpable spirit" of love, imagination.

In "Asphodel" Williams is still on the quest for wholeness dramatized in "The Wanderer"; he continues to search for Euridice. But in old age the images for absence or presence of the female beloved take on a lifetime of meaning; her presence becomes a matter of life or death.

"Asphodel," with its scope and depth, is primarily a love lyric. Euridice, not mentioned now, but still sought after in the imagination and in the flesh, is Flossie. In order to rescue her, Williams must himself be rescued; he needs his wife's forgiveness. Her compassion will help to restore him.

What power has love but forgiveness?
        In other words
                by its intervention
what has been done
          can be undone.
                 What good is it otherwise? (*PB*, 169)

Williams is poetically articulate with his new measure and emotionally articulate, able to make his plea. If Flossie can forgive him, not only will his "mind be cured" but the image of Persephone will be lifted from hell. The luminous marriage will be a sign of restitution.

C. Kerényi says of the Eleusinian mysteries that the first function of the ritual was to "perfect the world . . . in order that men might die more confidently after having lived better." "But," Kerényi continues, "the second condition was that men should also *know* about the happy marriage of the ravished Maiden—the prototype of all marriages. This knowledge was communicated to them by the beatific vision of Kore at Eleusis—vision of the innermost 'divine maiden' of men and women."[9]

In "Asphodel" Euridice is the living, human self whom the poet tries to redeem from death through art. In the triadic lines the imagination defies death, insisting that love will stay on through "abiding" song. The heart of the Eleusinian mysteries seems to have been a dramatization and a promise of rebirth.[10] Lyric poetry is not religious mystery, and yet Williams tells us that his poem concerns "every man / who wants to die at peace in his bed / besides" (*PB*, 162). Williams wrote "Asphodel" to keep his imagination alive and thereby to keep himself alive. The poem enriches our experience, giving us new memories, even if it will not make us live forever.

Persephone, the dark, elusive one, is also memory. "Asphodel" is about memory's power to renew experience, even as the poem is a quest for memory. Williams had had a severe

9. Kerényi, *Eleusis*, 174.
10. *Ibid.*, 93.

stroke in 1952, resulting in partial memory loss. Literally for the poet, "Memory is a kind / of accomplishment" (*PB*, 73), a return to life.

Early in the poem Williams speaks from the point of view of a ghost, a revenant. We remember how close he had come to death as a result of his recent illnesses. The living may "little prize" asphodel,

> but the dead see,
> > asking among themselves:
> What do I remember
> > that was shaped
> > > as this thing is shaped? (*PB*, 153)

Like the shaman, Williams hears the voices of spirits; he lets their questions inform him. "In the great night (his) heart will go out" to gather images of healing and renewal.[11] Williams brings himself back alive, giving emotion and at least a "wash of crimson," the tint of roses, to shapes that started out ghostly pale.[12]

The three-line stanzas of "Asphodel" move the images, accommodating the descent myth well. Each line is taut with both the descent, the return to memory, and the yearning for ascent, for the rescue from time. Though the poem has a narrative movement from the quest for love and speech to a resolution in the wedding song, the triadic lines incorporate descent and ascent in such a way that there is no separation of the two gestures or needs. The lines may descend on the page, but the music rises above them, an odor, Williams sings, "as from our wedding." Williams developed a poetry of "continual flowering" at the end of his life. "Each line or phrase"

11. This line comes from a "dream song" belonging to Owl Woman, a Papago healing woman. She said the chant was taught to her by the dead, to help her in her fight for the life of a sick man. One version of the song is found in William Brandon (ed.), *The Magic World: American Indian Songs and Poems* (New York, 1971), 42.

12. A handwritten note in the worksheets, found on the back of a typed page marked *Paterson, Book V: The River of Heaven*, refers to "the weak wash of crimson color" as the means "by which the rose is celebrated." YALC.

of the late poems "gathers the elements into inextricable union. Rising and sinking are not sequential but simultaneous."[13] The tension between descent and ascent is a "poised flower," which opens for Williams at the end of "Asphodel," in a release from time. For

> . . . love and the imagination
> > are of a piece,
> > > swift as the light
> > to avoid destruction.
> > > So we come to watch time's flight
> > > > as we might watch
> > summer lightning
> > > or fireflies, secure,
> > > > by grace of the imagination,
> > safe in its care. (*PB*, 179–80)

Williams' spirit rises from the ashes of his life's struggles to celebrate the light. He reduces time, the enemy, to size, and renders it not merely harmless but illuminating. As the poet rescues his world through love expressed in his art, he seems to observe the mysterious process of defeating ordinary time, as if its flight were occurring before him. An old man, and one who has long reflected on the imagination's powers, Williams is a spectator as well as a participant in his drama. The result of the poet's work is a sense of release, of imaginative freedom gained through the poetic line. The mythic pattern of descent can be translated into psychological terms. "According to depth psychologists, the two patterns of thinking [concerning Orpheus and Kora] are related and involved with the double. In 'Archetypes of the Collective Unconscious,' Carl Jung clears up some of the relationship by associating the Orphean descent with the archetype of the 'wise old man' or 'meaning.'"[14]

According to Jung, "'the Wise Old Man appears in dreams in the guise of a magician, doctor, priest, teacher, professor,

13. J. Hillis Miller, *Poets of Reality: Six Twentieth Century Writers* (Cambridge, Mass., 1966), 355.
14. Jerome Mazzaro, *William Carlos Williams: The Later Poems* (Ithaca, 1973), 15.

grandfather, or any other person possessing authority.'"[15] He appears the way Williams presents himself in "Asphodel," as the aging poet who comes to rescue the self in jeopardy. Jung sees the Wise Old Man as one who appears in dreams at a time of crisis to bring wholeness to a fragmented spirit. Williams performs this role for himself and his wife; he plays Demeter or Orpheus in the form of the Wise Old Man, a rescuer in his own voice. This time Williams draws upon the descent myth deliberately, to find and preserve imaginative treasures that might otherwise be lost forever. The old man descends, returns to his boyhood memories, returns to the present with a new sense of wholeness that defies time's blows. He gives this sense of wholeness as a gift in song to his wife.

The lines of "Asphodel" move like the chorus of an ancient drama, weaving back and forth in the dance of words. The truth of the measure goes back to the body's truth. As Williams says in *Kora*, "A thing known passes out of the mind into the muscles, the will is quit of it, save only when set into vibration by the forces of darkness opposed to it" (*K*, 71).

Jung has this to say about the creative, restorative quality of the descent undertaken with purpose; he hails those who "go down the sunset way with open eyes."

Things go very differently when the sacrifice is a voluntary one. Then it is no longer an overthrow, a "transvaluation of values," the destruction of all that we held sacred, but transformation and conservation. Everything young grows old, all beauty fades, all heat cools, all brightness dims, and every truth becomes stale and trite. For all these things have taken on shape, and all shapes are worn thin by the working of time; they age, sicken, crumble to dust—unless they change. But change they can, for the invisible spark that generated them is potent enough for infinite generation. No one should deny the danger of the descent, but it *can* be risked. No one *need* risk it, but it is certain that someone will. And let those who go down the sunset way do so with open eyes, for it is a sacrifice which daunts even the gods. Yet every descent is followed by an ascent; the vanishing shapes are shaped anew, and a truth is valid in the end

15. C. G. Jung, *Psyche and Symbol* (Garden City, 1952), 70–71. Quoted by Mazzaro, *William Carlos Williams: The Later Poems*, 16.

only if it suffers change and bears new witness in new images, in new tongues. . . .[16]

Within Jung's words we can also hear Williams' songs of descent; the poet trusts that there will be a corresponding ascent in his music if he can complete his journey.

The sources for "Asphodel" are the oldest sources of art, archaic; there are ancient and contemporary sources for the poem as well. In Book II the poet begins by "approaching death"; "place and condition," William's mainstays, begin to lose their particularity. He awakens as if from a bad dream. In order to prevent the shapes of things from growing dim, Williams advises us and himself:

> If we are to understand our time,
>   we must find the key to it,
>   not in the eighteenth
> and nineteenth centuries,
>   but in earlier, wilder
>   and darker epochs . .
> So to know, what I have to know
>   about my own death,
>   if it be real,
> I have to take it apart. (*PB*, 162–63)

To face death the poet must "dream back" to "darker epochs," to a time when myths of origin flourished. He must examine his suffering, "take it apart," as the tribal shaman had to experience a sense of dismemberment to render myth as a source of wholeness and new beginnings to his tribe.

Williams' journey takes the form of a dreaming back to early memories, to his childhood, and back deep into human memory, to see the shapes drawn on the walls "of prehistoric / caves in the Pyrenees" (*PB*, 174). The movement of dreaming back and of descent are one; both represent an inner voyage to the depths of the self, in a quest for origins. The poet takes us down the steps of the triadic line with him into the subway, where he exchanges glances with a man who reminds him of

16. C. G. Jung, *The Collected Works of C. G. Jung*, trans. R. F. C. Hull, Bollingen Series XX, Vol. 5: *Symbols of Transformation* (Princeton, 1956), 357.

his father. And the subway with its modern power jolts open the image of archaic caves, places that reveal the emergence of human consciousness and the origins of art.

Williams refers to the fact that Paleolithic shamanic artists "left their marks, / by torchlight," for the regions in which they painted were deep in the earth (*PB*, 174). Their art "was done deep down in the darkest and most dangerous parts of the caves, although the men lived only in the openings of the caves."[17] Most people live at the surface ("Look at / what passes for the new") but the poet goes deeper to provide for us; the passage down is tortuous. By going deep into the earth and creating animals in paint, the early draftsmen must have gained power over the animals, as Williams seeks to find words that will capture his most profound emotional stirrings and make the emotions vibrant in the dance of the poem. This hunt requires all of the poet's artistry.

Within the Paleolithic caves of Cantabria archeologists have found extraordinary figurines of the Great Mother as well as images of bison, of the hunt. At this point in his poem, having faced death and moved beyond it to the theme of love's forgiveness, the poet finds himself in depths that resonate with masculine and feminine powers, powers of creativity, fertility. Williams acknowledges the two principles.

> Their women
>   had big buttocks.
>   But what
> draftsmen they were!
>   By my father's beard,
>   what draftsmen. (*PB*, 174)

The cave paintings, like early Chinese drawings and paintings, were not an expression of facile simplicity, but of craft and design. From 40,000 B.C. to the present day "there have been great numbers of primitive peoples living throughout the world, yet none has had a representational art to ap-

---

17. Robert J. Braidwood, *Prehistoric Man* (Chicago, 1967), 72.

proach that of [the Paleolithic cave-painters]."[18] How could Williams not have felt a kinship with images "from the hands of men who knew the great animals well—knew the feel of their fur, the tremendous drive of their muscles, and the danger one faced when he hunted them"?[19] Williams had always respected artists who knew their materials and recognized things with a "glandular perception of their uniqueness." At the end of Book III his poem touches the first traces of humanness, with a source that revels in the particularities of art. The newspapers may carry the terrible news of the burning of "priceless Goyas" by Perón's goons, but the paintings on the cave walls, the memory of the origins of art, remain intact and living for the poet.[20]

On his dangerous journey Williams carries "torchlight" in the image of the flower. Having missed contact with him, the man on the subway is "a flower / whose savor had been lost." The cave drawings have not lost their savor, they are "lilacs" left by the archaic draftsmen (*PB*, 174). As in tribal poetry, where through repetition and association of imagery one image brings together the cosmos and is used to explore it in all its sacred ramifications, Williams uses the flower image both as a center and as a place of change.[21]

Out of the flower, or memory of his father and of the "great fathers" resting within the mountain beds, Williams creates a world:

> in a subway train
>   I build a picture
>   of all men. (*PB*, 174)

18. Jacquetta Hawkes, *Prehistory* (New York, 1963), 286.

19. Braidwood, *Prehistoric Man*, 72. For a provocative personal and poetic exploration of the drawings in prehistoric caves (and for an argument against seeing these figures as mere depictions of the hunt), see Clayton Eshleman's *Hades in Manganese* (Santa Barbara, 1981).

20. New York *Times*, April 16, 1953, Sec. 1, p. 4. This event took place two days before Williams' release from the mental hospital.

21. See the Vedic hymn "To the God of Fire as a Horse" and the Navajo "Night Chant" as two examples among many in *Technicians of the Sacred*, ed. Jerome Rothenberg (New York, 1965), 44, 79.

Williams reminds us that the poem brings its life to the present. Yet like the earth diver in tribal mythology, the poet goes deep for materials with which to begin again. The poem's journey, like the earth-diver myth, reinforces the singer's identity, that of the "mythopoeic male." Through his contact with origins, the poet revitalizes an image of himself as a creator, as a man who gives birth.[22]

The descent myth that recurs in Williams' poems is universal and need not refer to specific tribal mythologies. Yet Williams does open the book *Pictures from Brueghel* with a quotation about tribal practices: "'. . . the form of a man's rattle may be in accordance with instructions received in the dream by which he obtained his power'" (Frances Densmore, *The Study of Indian Music*). Williams was an accomplished dreamer.

Frazer's *Golden Bough*, with its descriptions of ancient myths and rituals, comes to mind when one reads "Asphodel, That Greeny Flower." As indicated in chapter 3, Williams takes the image of the flower with him throughout his poetry as a protection against chaos, reminiscent of the way that Aeneas carried the golden bough through Hades as a protection against death. Frazer's account of why Virgil chose the mistletoe or golden bough for Aeneas, accurate or not, is lyrical and suggestive for our comments on Williams' use of flower imagery. Frazer says of the mistletoe that "its fiery nature marks it out, on homeopathic principles, as the best possible cure or prevention of injury by fire. . . ." Frazer continues, "If the mistletoe, as a yellow withered bough in the sad autumn woods, was conceived to contain the seed of fire, what better companion could a forlorn wanderer in the nether shades take with him than a bough that would be a lamp to his feet as well as a rod and a staff to his hands? Armed with it he might boldly confront the dreadful spectres that would cross his path on his adventurous journey."[23] For Williams, the "yellow flower"

22. Alan Dundes, "Earth-Diver: Creation of the Mythopoeic Male," *American Anthropologist*, LXIV (October, 1962), 1032–48.
23. Sir James George Frazer, *The Golden Bough* (1922; rpr. New York, 1972), 819.

or "sacred flower" (*PB*, 89) of any color to match the poet's mood is his emblem for art's power to bring the poet safely through the hell of his experience. The triadic line, the measure, is the solid "rod and staff" that Williams uses to hold off time and his own terror. Unlike *Paterson*, which "refuses to claim a center,"[24] "Asphodel" has a formal center that permits the poet to take a dangerous journey, and to dance.

24. Joseph N. Riddel, *The Inverted Bell: Modernism and the Counterpoetics of William Carlos Williams* (Baton Rouge, 1974), 186.

CHAPTER SIX

A Journey with the Ancients and the Moderns

For the modern poet the image serves the protective, restorative function provided for Aeneas by the golden bough. Art serves an archetypal function as a shield, to permit the artist to voyage through dangerous realms and to explore them, without destruction to the seer.[1] The image is Williams' shining flower; the flower is his most frequently used image for seeing, for perceiving without being shattered. As Williams says, flowers have the "prerogative" of renewal. In *Kora* the bouquet is seen as a mark of the turning point from descent to ascent, and as a protection for the next round of experience. "Then at the sickening turn toward death the pieces are joined into a pretty thing, a bouquet frozen in an ice-cake. *This* is art, *mon cher*, a thing to carry up with you on the next turn . . ." (*K*, 67).

We know that Williams was familiar with Frazer's *Golden Bough*, for he mentions it in *Paterson*, Book II: "You also, I am sure, have read / Frazer's Golden Bough" (*P*, 92). Williams speaks of the work as if its contents are common knowledge; he refers to Frazer's work in the context of expressing awe before a lover's beauty, and terror before sacrifice.

1. Maud Bodkin, *Archetypal Patterns in Poetry: Psychological Studies of Imagination* (London, 1968), 130–36.

But for a description of Aeneas' travels with the golden bough, Williams would not have had to go to Frazer. Williams knew *The Aeneid* well. We find implicit references to that epic throughout "Asphodel," from the echo in the opening line to some of the dramatic passages of narrative.[2] The echo in "Asphodel" of Aeneas' meeting with Dido in hell is perhaps more obvious than the echo of (and contrast with) the scene in Book V of *The Aeneid*, where Aeneas meets his father, Anchises, in the underworld. In Book III of "Asphodel" Williams tells of an episode in the modern underworld, the subway, where he sees a man who looks like his father but misses the opportunity to speak with him. Aeneas did meet his father in the underworld; Anchises welcomed him.

> So you have come at last? The love that your
> father relied on
> Has won through the hard journey? And may I
> gaze, my son,
> Upon your face, and exchange the old homely
> talk with you?[3]

In his own lack of contact with his father, with other men, Williams feels his isolation as a modern poet. With the loss of contact he seems to lose the future, the prophetic gifts.

> Speak to him,
> I cried. He
> will know the secret.
> He was gone
> and I did nothing about it.
> With him
> went all men
> and all women too
> were in his loins. (*PB*, 173–74)

"Fanciful or not," Williams experiences a sense of loss. He is left to create on his own, to "build a picture / of all men," of their loss of contact and their yearning to renew the power of

2. Williams' lines echo Virgil's opening lines: "Arma virum que cano" (Of arms and the man I sing).

3. Virgil, *The Aeneid*, trans. C. Day Lewis (Garden City, 1953), 150.

communication. Loss is only one stage in this "journey to love," to healing.

Williams' use of materials from epic poetry, his admiration for Homer that shows up so clearly in "Asphodel," indicate that it is doubtful that the poem "must be regarded first as a kind of reply to Eliot, Pound, and Dante. . . ."[4] Although Williams is always concerned with being a modern poet ("How shall I be a mirror to this modernity?"—*CEP*, 3), "Asphodel" is also Williams' attempt to equal the greatness of the old epics. In his late years Williams identifies more with Homer than with Pound. Throughout Williams' essays and letters and *Autobiography* he expresses an admiration for Homer and a determination "not to write in a lesser mode" than any of the great writers of the past (*SE*, "Preface," n.p.).

Williams admired Homer's gift for capturing ordinary, popular speech. He also admired Homer's detachment, which he himself sought to emulate. "It is the poet's detachment that is the spring, Homer himself is unaffected" (*SE*, 277).

In the last essay on "Measure" Williams includes a section on Chapman's translation of Homer, in which he enthusiastically praises Chapman's version of *The Iliad*. In fact, Williams seems to be talking about himself when he speaks of Chapman's work, for Williams too sought a "sea-beat" for his work in the last poems. Williams admires Chapman's work as a young translator but seems to identify more with Chapman as he grows older. ". . . When he [Chapman] returned to the work at his prime he was a very different man than he had been at the start. He showed himself to have a deeper understanding of the poet's role. Homer's poem had entered and become part of him."[5]

Williams admires Chapman for breaking away from iambic pentameter and working with a variable line, as he himself did in his last years. Williams says of Chapman's lines that

4. "Pearce's *The Continuity of American Poetry* rightly suggests that 'Asphodel's' invention must be regarded first as a kind of reply to Eliot, Pound and Dante. . . ." Jerome Mazzaro, *William Carlos Williams: The Later Poems* (Ithaca, 1973), 95.

5. "Measure: —a loosely assembled essay on poetic measure," 20. YALC.

they "show a variety and resourcefulness which is almost infinite. . . ." This variety "comes from something hidden, embedded in the idiom itself," as Williams sees the measure of the triadic line embedded in the American idiom. Chapman, according to Williams, worked instinctively and succeeded so well because he "became Homer as he warmed to his task."

Williams applauds Chapman's courage and hard work; he respects these qualities in his own work as well, as we can hear in the praise of Chapman: "Chapman gave up the pentameter, as far as he had the guts for it, and struggled into the new measure. That it was a struggle is marked in everything he had to do. The effect was electric!" Williams goes on to quote from Chapman's translation of *The Iliad* and comments, "That's straight talking," the kind of straight talking that Homer had originally effected, and that Williams himself worked to achieve.[6]

Williams' *Autobiography*, begun in 1948 and published in 1951, opens with a section entitled "First Memories." The second line of the *Autobiography*, written in 1948, begins, "Only yesterday, reading Chapman's *The Iliad of Homer* . . ." (*A*, 3). References to Homer and his works recur in prominent places throughout Williams' writing. Not Pound first, or even Dante, but Homer.

In his letters, Williams refers to his readings of Rouse's translation of *The Iliad* and *The Odyssey* during his recovery from his illnesses in the early 1950s. He read *The Iliad* in 1951, during his hospital stay. Williams borrowed the classics from his neighbor at the shore in Connecticut, a Professor Stecchini, professor of Greek and Latin. Williams commented on the fatefulness of this contact with his neighbor. "I have read the *Odyssey*; I borrowed it from the Stecchinis. . . . Isn't it strange that I should now be so much interested in these classic books and then blindly run smack into a classic scholar at the shore in Connecticut?" (*SL*, 307).

While severely ill from the strokes, Williams found that he admired Homer's works all the more for the clarity and re-

6. *Ibid.*, 21, 23, 24.

solve before death he found depicted there. The poet writes to Frank V. Moore of a "carved East Indian mask" that reminds him of the mood of *The Iliad*.

I saw it last night while I was sitting listening to some music. It came to life, complacent before death, complete peace. It was a lesson to me—and no dogma to soften the blow. It had the peace before violent death that is in the *Iliad*, and the consciousness, the complete consciousness, before it that is in the heroes of Greek legend. . . .

To copy nature is a spineless activity. . . . But to imitate nature involves the verb. . . . The *Iliad* is a pure invention; the *Odyssey* is another. The *Divine Comedy* is another, though I reject it for the mist it invents to hide death from the eye. . . . In the *Iliad* the air is clear; there is no interested fog between the words and the senses. (*SL*, 297–98)

The Iliad gave Williams personal strength and inspiration for the writing of "Asphodel." Though Williams admired Pound's work, we do not hear of Williams turning to the *Cantos* during his time of crisis.

In "Asphodel" Williams tells the reader how important *The Iliad* is to him, whereas he makes no direct mention of the influence of Pound or Eliot. Williams sings of the "nostalgic sea" (*P*, 235) that is an imaginative home.

> The sea! The sea!
>   Always
>   when I think of the sea
>   there comes to mind
>   the *Iliad*
>   and Helen's public fault
>   that bred it. (*PB*, 158)

Williams speaks as if *The Iliad* were the source of all poetry. Indeed, in the worksheets for "Asphodel" Williams instructs Flossie and the reader, "All poems stem from / the *Iliad* . . . / repeat it!"[7]

In Book I of "Asphodel" Williams makes a comparison of his work with that of Homer.

7. Worksheets for "Asphodel," page marked 23, beginning "There is a piece of sculpture." YALC.

Begin again.
          It is like Homer's
                    catalogue of ships:
     it fills up time. (*PB,* 159)

Williams' "catalogue" is one of flowers and gardens, yet be-
neath the flower imagery the same "profound depth" of sea,
of universal imagination that launched Homer's epic moves
Williams' lines.

In his old age Williams identifies with the figure of Homer,
the prophet and bard.

                         Death is no answer,
     no answer—
              to a blind old man
                    whose bones
          have the movement
              of the sea,
                    a sexless old man
          for whom it is a sea
              of which his verses
                    are made up. (*PB,* 166)

Williams has become one with the rhythm of his poem. Where
the river entered his heart in "The Wanderer," now a more
vast and universal movement enters his bones.

Asphodel, the flower that launches Williams' poem, is found
in Homer's Hades, Book XI of *The Odyssey.* W. H. D. Rouse includes mention of the flower as part of the fields of the dead
in his prose translation; so does Fitzgerald in his more contemporary verse translation. Chapman speaks of a "herbie
mead" and does not mention asphodel. Williams must have
had Rouse's translation close by, or in mind, when writing
"Asphodel." As Rouse translates, "Then the ghost of spring-
heel Achilles marched away with long steps over the meadow
of asphodel. . . ."[8] There are implicit references to at least two

8. Homer, *The Story of Odysseus,* trans. W. H. D. Rouse (London and Edin-
burgh, 1945), 129; Homer, *The Odyssey,* trans. Robert Fitzgerald (Garden City,
1963), 202; Homer, *The Odyssey and the Lesser Homerica,* trans. Chapman (New
York, 1956), 204.

epics in the opening lines of "Asphodel." But Williams comes to sing of a personal matter.

The descent myth in "Asphodel" is personal, introspective, a drama of memory that reminds us of the work of other modern authors. A critical work on modern poetry can hardly speak of renewal of spirit through memory and art without reference to Bergson, Proust, or Baudelaire. Perhaps Williams' critics do not mention these figures central to modern literature because of the lack of direct influence on Williams. Then, too, there has been an attempt among most critics to keep Williams American.[9] Williams himself said, "The French poets have had no influence on me whatever—unless it be something so occult and subtle that I myself have been unaware of it" (*SL*, 119). Williams protests too much. He does admit to the influence of "the French spirit, which, through my mother, is partly my own." (Williams' mother was half-French, from Mayaguez, and studied art in Paris before marrying Mr. Williams.)

The spirit of the writings of Bergson, Proust, and Baudelaire pervades modern literature, and Williams had to have absorbed some of that spirit. When Williams praises the lyrical novels of Joyce in his essays, he does not acknowledge that Proust preceded Joyce in making of literature into a world. Williams overlooked this influence of Proust on Joyce's lyrical novel because Williams was so taken with Joyce's technical innovations, with his breaking down of the usual structures of speech and recreating a new world in literature.

We find no mention of Bergson in Williams' writings, but there are notes on Proust in the *Essays*; furthermore, there are passages in Williams' writings that bear a remarkable affinity with others in *A la recherche du temps perdu*. In the essay "Revelation" (1947), Williams distorts Proust somewhat in order to make his own point. According to Williams, "Proust dug back

9. Bram Dijkstra's excellent collection of essays by Williams, *A Recognizable Image: William Carlos Williams on Art and Artists* (New York, 1978), is an antidote to this misunderstanding of Williams; the book shows Williams' cosmopolitanism in his writings about the universals in art, as well as his appreciation of American art.

into his mind for something, something lost, mind what I say, something lost. It was lost and he did not, definitely he did not, find it any more than Rousseau found it in his *Confessions*. Both men are moralists . . . saying . . . Stop maiming the times! . . . We do not like our deformity. Look what might have been!" (*SE*, 271). Williams does not acknowledge that Proust felt that he had recovered more than what was lost, that the narrator had had a revelation of art's powers at the end of the great work. He distorts Proust's role as a moralist in order to make his own point, that in the present we are starved for "actual values," not those imposed by a dogmatic and rigid society.

Williams, for all his emphasis on memory in his old age, still has more of a belief in the present as a source of reality than Proust had. Williams savors the present moment even as he savors memories in his last poems.

In "The Poem as a Field of Action" (1948) Williams mentions Proust's work in another context, where he acknowledges the radical impact of Proust's work, points to his writings as a source of possibilities. In this essay Williams speaks of the impact of the atom bomb on modern consciousness. "For one great thing about 'the bomb' is the awakened sense it gives us that catastrophic . . . alterations are also possible in the human *mind*, in art, in the arts . . . it is *possible*." If the physicists can effect such terrific changes in human life, so can the artists, Williams implies. Williams makes this note to himself, after his reading of Edmund Wilson's *Axel's Castle*: "Note: *Proust*: (Wilson) He has supplied for the first time in literature an equivalent on the full scale for the new theory of modern physics—I mention this merely to show a possible relationship—between a style and a natural science—intelligently considered" (*SE*, 287).

Here we see that the influence of Proust is not direct, but transmitted to Williams through criticism. Williams does not go on to explain his point further, but the implication seems to be that a theory of art and its effect on style can have as drastic and far-reaching an impact on the human mind as the discovery of nuclear theory and the resulting weapons. Art, too, can restructure life, can change our way of seeing. Proust taught his readers to appreciate the redeeming power of "involuntary memory," as the artist reconstructed it into beauty in his work.

Proust's belief in "involuntary memory" would seem to be in contrast with Williams' faith in *work* at memory, in deliberate attempts to evoke redeeming memories, as in "Asphodel." Yet there are passages in Williams' *Autobiography* that sound very close to passages from Proust's *A la recherche du temps perdu*. Though there may be no direct influence, the affinity is striking. Williams speaks of the great comfort and pleasure that he has always derived from flowers, "a half-ashamed pleasure," he says. "The slender neck of the anemone particularly haunts me. . . . My curiosity in these things was unbounded—secret, certainly. There is a long history in each of us that comes as not only a reawakening but a repossession when confronted by this world" (*A*, 19). This last statement about "repossession" or recapturing might have been written by Proust.[10] Williams' secret pleasure in the sensual details of the flowers reminds us of Proust's young narrator, as he walks among the hawthorn flowers along "Swann's Way," as he loses himself, in secret ecstacy amid the odor and rhythm of the flowers.[11]

Asphodel, the pressed, ghostly flower of Williams' poem, reminds us of the dried lime flowers made into an "infusion de thé ou de tilleul" for Proust's young narrator by "tante Léonie." These dried lime flowers, with the madeleine, awaken the narrator's memory life, start him on his quest to understand the secret of his ecstatic feelings. When Proust sums up his feelings after the tea and madeleine, the insights of the older narrator sound like a description of the mood of Williams' poem "Asphodel."

10. Williams read *Axel's Castle* and wrote this section of his *Autobiography* within weeks of each other, "early in 1948, while recovering from a heart attack." Note to the author from Paul Mariani, December 6, 1980.

11. Marcel Proust, *A la recherche du temps perdu* (3 vols.; Paris, 1954), I, 138–39.

Mais, quand d'un passé ancien rien ne subsiste, après la mort des êtres, après la destruction des choses, seules, plus frêles mais plus vivaces, plus immatérielles, plus persistantes, plus fidèles, l'odeur et la saveur restent encore longtemps, comme des âmes, à se rappeler, à attendre, à espérer, sur la ruine de tout le reste, à porter sans fléchir, sur leur gouttelette presque impalpable, l'édifice immense du souvenir.

"Asphodel" builds an extended, if not "immense structure of memory," from the memory of the small pressed flowers; and the world reawakened or repossessed in "Asphodel" through memory has a music or a "measure" that is timeless, like the regenerating "phrase of music" that Proust's Swann so loved.[12]

The word *souvenir* is also used frequently in Baudelaire's poetry—perhaps the only word used more often is *esprit*. Though Williams denied the influence of French poets on his work, when Williams says "there were flowers also / in hell" (*PB*, 153), we cannot help but remember that Williams was not the first poet to be aware that beauty can be culled from suffering and from cruelty. In his early notes for "Asphodel" Williams refers to asphodel as "a sort of mental flower" (YALC), much as Baudelaire's "flowers of evil" are a reflection of the poet's consciousness of his memories.[13] The creative, reconstructive introspection that one finds in Proust, in Baudelaire, in Williams' late love poetry, is a modern kind of "descent" and return with treasure.

12. *Ibid.*, 47, 210–11.
13. Charles Baudelaire, *Les Fleurs du Mal* in *Oeuvres complètes* (Paris, 1961).

CHAPTER SEVEN

Fluid Speaking: The Worksheets

The worksheets for "Asphodel" are deeply moving to anyone who is seriously interested in writing or reading poetry. In the rough drafts we see a poet at the height of his technical powers, a man who is physically in pain and quite weak, scratching away to save his life.[1] Williams' workings on the poem remind us of how close a poem in process can come to not being a poem at all; of how much skill and patience Williams showed in the writing and rewriting of "Asphodel," so that he finally could say what he wanted to say. We find many changes in the text as it progresses; mainly these are deletions that improve the style, tone, and texture of the poem. But in the deletions we overhear Williams expressing some of his deepest feelings. In one of the three typed versions of Book III ("What power has love but forgiveness?") Williams writes,

> To bridge that gap
> is our affair
> by what training I have
> in the skills of my art
> remains my final purpose.
> It is to be loved by you
> and to be sure of it

1. "Paterson: Book V" (Worksheets, YALC). Unless otherwise noted, references in this chapter are to these YALC worksheets.

        faulty as you are
                as the whole human race is faulty
                        that I have persisted.

The gap Williams speaks of bridging, in the context of his notes for the poem, is between love and lovelessness, speech and speechlessness, seeing and vision, life and death. That he worked under emotional pressure and the pressure of failing physical forces as he worked on "Asphodel" is evident from the notes, though we do not hear self-involvement in the polished poem. There is pathos and heroism in Williams' desire "to be sure" that he would be heard and be loved; that he would "cure" the mind of deathly fears, maybe even of death. He felt that he was working for the whole "faulty" human race.

In Williams' handwritten notes to himself on the worksheets we hear something close to prayer; there is at least a kind of pleading in the language that the work may succeed and be "sure." There is anger as well, anger at Flossie, a stress on failures that was best left out of a poem of reconciliation. In this chapter of our study we look at the worksheets or diary for the poem that became "Asphodel, That Greeny Flower." We follow Williams' plunge into the "rhythmic ebb and flow" of his imagination and his emergence with a clearly shaped poem.

Williams used the formal orderliness of "Asphodel" to help make the poem into one of discovery; work on this poem strengthened Williams' powers as a poet. The fact that Williams moved on to other forms than the triadic line in his last poems, *Pictures from Brueghel* and *Paterson V*, does not mean that "Asphodel" was any sort of failure. Williams had to keep on changing and growing in his style, to stay flexible and to stay alive in mind. In order to see how the poem is a voyage of discovery, the reader must try to enter into the drama of the poem itself, and into its creation.

In his essay "How to Write" (1936), Williams speaks of the depths of personality that can be reached through the poem:

Today we know the meaning of depth, it is a primitive profundity of the personality that must be touched if what we do is to have it. The

faculties, untied, proceed backward through the night of our unconscious past. It goes down to the ritualistic, amoral past of the race, to
fetish, to dream to wherever the "genius" of the particular writer
finds itself able to go.
    At such time the artist (the writer) may well be thought of as a
dangerous person. (*Int*, 97)

The "demonic power of the mind," its depth and ability to
touch universal sources, is found in rhythm—"it is the rhythmic ebb and flow of the mysterious life process and unless
this is tapped by the writer nothing of moment can result. It is
the reason for the value of poetry whose unacknowledged
rhythmic symbolism is its greatest strength and which makes
all prose in comparison with it little more than the patter of
the intelligence" (*Int*, 98). Williams' emphasis on measure, his
excitement over the variable foot, occurred because the poet
saw the new measure as a tool for sounding the depths, renewing the "rhythmic symbolism" of verse.
    After the writing has been done, Williams says, it is "no
longer a fluid speaking through a symbolism of ritualistic
forms" but an object for the critical scrutiny of the poet, who
must now apply critical intelligence. Williams complains that
this second stage of writing is all that academic literary critics
understand and concern themselves with. "It is this part of
writing that is dealt with in the colleges and in all forms of
teaching but nowhere does it seem to be realized that without
its spring from the deeper strata of the personality all the
teaching and learning in the world can make nothing of the
result. Not to have realized this is the greatest fault of those
who think they know something of the art" (*Int*, 98–99).
    A way to take the voyage with Williams through the "fluid
speaking" of "Asphodel" is to examine the worksheets for the
long poem found in the Yale American Library Collection. As
Sherman Paul states, after his consideration of the long poem
"The Desert Music," "The poem, of course is adequate in itself. . . . But the manuscript versions are part of the drama of
the poem and should be worked through as part of the reading of the poem—for the sake of the sometimes prosaic clarity

(and confirmation) of the original material and for a just sense of the many transformations and realizations achieved by Williams' art."[2]

Before commenting on changes that Williams made on "Asphodel" in the worksheet version, I will describe the materials for the reader who does not have access to the early version. The worksheets for "Asphodel," including seventy pages, can be found in the Yale collection under the heading *Paterson V*. One of the first elements of the drama of Williams' work that the researcher notices is that the poet began "Asphodel" thinking that he was writing *Paterson V*. Yet the poem to Flossie developed into a poem in its own right, a rich, intimate world. With its difference in emphasis, Williams dedicated *Book V* of the published version of *Paterson* to art, "To the / Memory / of / HENRI TOULOUSE LAUTREC, / *Painter*" (*P*, 240).

Most of the worksheets with versions of "Asphodel" are typed. They were written after Williams' second severe stroke, typed on an electric typewriter with the left hand. Often we find notes added to the worksheets in pencil; words are inserted into lines or marked in the margins. There are a few pages of notes handwritten in pencil. Most of the penciled-in notes are difficult to decipher; the handwriting is very scraggly. The penciled marks look as if they were written by a shaky hand; probably they were written in with the left hand. From the worksheets we can appreciate how difficult it must have been for Williams to accomplish the mechanics of getting the poem on paper.

The worksheets contain almost a full set of pages of the three books that we find in the published version of "Asphodel." The "Coda" is missing from the worksheets. The pages are not a polished version, but a working one, with additions and deletions. Besides two pages of handwritten notes on the nature of "asphodel," there are three attempts at an opening page, each marked with a different heading. One page titled

2. Sherman Paul, *The Music of Survival: A Biography of a Poem by William Carlos Williams* (Urbana, 1968), 132, n. 2.

"(*for Flossie*)" and marked "(dialogue)" in pencil appears to be a very early version. Another attempt to begin the poem is titled "*Paterson, Book V: The River of Heaven*" and includes two typed pages. The last version is titled "(for Flossie)" and is marked "*Paterson V,*—a beginning" in pencil. This version includes twenty-one pages; some of the material was later placed in Book II in the published version.

In the final version of "Asphodel" Williams does not include Flossie's name, or the names of any of his friends. (Marsden Hartley's name appears in the rough draft and is deleted.) The decision to make the poem intimate, yet not exclusive, seems to be a wise one. That the poem did not want to be a part of *Paterson V,* that it had a life of its own as a love poem written in the long triadic lines, must have become evident to Williams only after he had worked on the poem for quite a while. Perhaps Williams realized the poem's uniqueness after he had published Book I of "Asphodel" as "Work in Progress" in the 1954 volume of *Journey to Love*.[3]

There are no dates or consistent page numbers on the worksheets, so we can decide which are the earliest attempts only by noting how the poem progresses in stages toward the final, published version. There is a section of Book III in the worksheets marked "first version," and this section includes several different attempts at passages within Book III. Also, we find a section marked Section III, beginning "We shall not live forever," which includes five pages of material not included in the final version. A helpful date within the worksheets can be found on a menu dated Saturday, March 1, 1952. On the front of the menu Williams began to take some notes as to what the flower asphodel might mean.

Critics who have studied Williams' worksheets for other poems usually point out that the poet's revisions lead to con-

3. See Paul Mariani's discussion of the evolution of "Asphodel" in his article "The Whore/Virgin and the Wounded One-Horned Beast," *Denver Quarterly*, XIII (Summer, 1978), 109. Mariani suggests that the working title "River of Heaven" refers back to *Paterson IV*, to a letter by Allen Ginsberg, incorporated into the poem. Ginsberg speaks of River Street in Paterson as being "at the heart of what is to be known" (*P*, 228).

ciseness. Cutting and paring for clarity is exactly what we would expect to find in Williams' worksheets, after reading his letters and essays. And we do find a lot of trimming of extra materials in the worksheets for "Asphodel." But we discover more about Williams' technique as a poet from his worksheets than that he is economical with language. For one thing, we must look to see where he cut, what kinds of materials, for what effect. Williams deletes words not only for the sake of tightening a line, making it more sparse, but also to eliminate dogmatism or didactic language. He leaves out whole sections of subject matter in order to achieve a balanced version of the final poem. We find that Williams not only deletes materials, but he adds words as well, to achieve subtlety, fluidity, and the sense of intimacy that we have admired. Most interesting of all, we find in Williams' worksheets a kind of diary of the process of writing. The poet questions himself about the work at hand; we see that he is discovering much of his content as he works. Williams' handwritten notes are particularly moving in this respect as the poet makes comments to himself about his subject, about the craft of poetry.

Throughout the worksheets we can find examples of places where Williams has deleted and changed phrases to achieve a tightened and more dramatic final version. We can see the striking effect of Williams' cutting and sharpening in the last version of Book II, where Williams includes a page of verse that is easy to read since it is unmarked:

>   There is something urgent
>   I have to say to you
>   and you alone
>   but it must wait
>   while I enjoy
>   the pleasure,
>   the rare pleasure,
>   of approach
>   which I am not sure
>   may ever come again
>   and so
>   I drag it out

with fear in my heart
            and keep on talking
                        for I dare not stop
forgive me
            if I drag out the pleasure.
                        Listen
while I talk on against time,
            I will not be
                        too long.
I have forgot

The inclusion in the rough draft copy of "while I enjoy / the pleasure, / the rare pleasure, / of approach / which I am not sure may ever come again" destroys the effect of urgency that Williams achieved in the final, published version.

            There is something
                        something urgent
I have to say to you
            and you alone
                        but it must wait
while I drink in
            the joy of your approach,
                        perhaps for the last time. (*PB*, 154)

Cutting away the repeated phrases about "pleasure" and using the shorter word "joy" makes the statement more direct. "Pleasure" called too much attention to the speaker, while the final version establishes a balance, a dialogue between the speaker and the "you" in the poem. "Wait while I drink in" as one line holds the reader in suspense, and yet the line moves quickly; "drink in" has a more exact meaning and a more absorbing effect than "while I enjoy." "Perhaps for the last time" is shorter and more emphatic an ending to the passage than the wordy "which I am not sure / may ever come again."

Another place in the poem where Williams makes a deletion that tightens the lines and makes them more direct, dramatic rather than explanatory, occurs in pages that will be part of Book II in the final version (marked as page 21 of Book I in the rough draft). The worksheet version reads as follows:

> Every drill driven into the earth
> upon
> our irreplaceable treasures in oil
> enters as well,
> my side. Waste, waste!

The published version reads:

> Every drill
> driven into the earth
> for oil enters my side
> also.
> Waste, waste! (*PB*, 168)

The effect of cutting "upon / our irreplacable treasures" is to make the lines move into one another more abruptly, to convey the effect of the drill moving into the poet's side. In the final version the poet manages to keep "enters my side" as one phrase, which helps the words make an impression of directness. This effect is important, for through language Williams wants to make the universe into a personal phenomenon that the reader can feel and take responsibility for.

Throughout the worksheets Williams deletes phrases that sounded too expository or dogmatic. This category of deletions and changes adds to a unity of effect through the tone of the poem; the original version sounds at times like a lecture; the final poem is a love song.

In the first two drafts of page one, Williams uses phrases which sound very much like the opening remarks for a class. In "(for Flossie)" he says, ". . . Today I've come / to talk to you about those flowers / that we both loved." The second attempt reads almost the same way: "So today I've come / to talk to you about them—of flowers." This kind of explicit and formal announcing of purpose is eliminated from the third draft attempt, which sings, "I come, my sweet, / to sing to you." Quite an improvement! A changeover from the Old Professor to the poet as lover and singer.

The earliest versions of page one also contain an explanatory statement about "asphodel," beginning with the demonstrative pronoun "that": "Of asphodel, that greeny flower, / that is a simple flower." This second line is eliminated in the third revision, which reads like the published version. The deletion of the explanatory note helps to make the poem evocative, not explicit, while adding also to the rolling, musical quality of the opening lines.

That Williams had a didactic purpose in mind originally is evident from an early passage the poet crossed out with a large penciled X:

> I put you
>   in my class to instruct
>   in what I am
>   so that you may forgive me.

This kind of didacticism would have put off the reader, and Flossie, surely. We do not wish to be "put to school" by the poet. The final version of the poem invites, appeals to the reader and to Flossie to listen and participate.

In the published poem the poet still makes it clear that he wishes to teach his wife to see into the nature of his experience, so that she may understand and forgive him. There may still be a slight note of condescension, but the poet's approach is much more gentle than the rough-draft version. He invokes the name of love; he asks his wife's permission to speak on.

> In the name of love
>   I come proudly
>   as to an equal
>   to be forgiven.
>   Let me, for I know
>   you take it hard,
>   with good reason,
>   give the steps
>   if it may be
>   by which you shall mount,
>   again to think well
>   of me. (*PB*, 170–71)

As Paul Mariani writes, "His wife's generosity in forgiving him is not enough. She must also see what he sees." Williams is the "teacher" in this poem, "garnering the fruits of his epic journey, crafty Odysseus retelling his tale to Penelope."[4]

Williams leaves out long passages and even whole pages of material from the worksheets in the finished version. Some of the material Williams chooses to leave out might be considered self-pitying or self-serving. The omission of the reference to his illness found in the rough-draft version shows us that Williams chose to follow an aesthetic ethic of leaving himself out of the poem. The persona in "Asphodel" is personal, direct, the voice of the poet that expresses love, fear of time, hope for his wife's generosity and understanding, and belief in art's power to keep the memory of love alive. Williams leaves out the following passage, which would have called too much attention to his person and detracted from his song (the passage would have occurred in Book II after "I lived / to breathe above the stench"):

> I gave freely
> what I had to give.
> Latterly the accident of my illness
> stopped that.
> Or not
> unless you ignore
> the poem
> and all that it holds to me.

The omission of this passage in the final version makes the poem tighter in the movement of its lines where Williams simply states "I was lost / failing the poem" (*PB*, 164). The movement of the poem goes on with a line about reemergence from the sea. The poet's omission here may have had to do with judgment about suitable content, not just with the art of cutting and sharpening for clarity.

On the same worksheet page (marked 15) Williams crossed out a reference to his parents and to what they had taught him. The worksheet version is too allusive.

4. Paul Mariani, "The Satyr's Defense: Williams' 'Asphodel,'" *Contemporary Literature*, XIV (1973), 10, 7.

                The deaths I suffered
                        in contrast,
        began as well,
                with the eyes I got from my parents.
                        They were too alert,
        too keen,
                not to see through
                        the world's niggardliness. . . .

Williams crossed out "in contrast," and "I got"; he added
"and the heart," so that the fourth line would have read "with
the eyes and the heart from my parents." The meaning in the
published version is very clear.

        The deaths I suffered
                began in the heads
                        about me, my eyes
        were too keen
                not to see through
                        the world's niggardliness. (*PB*, 164)

The poet decided that the reference to his parents was unnecessary. Without mention of the family, the final version is
more assertive.

    Williams decided to omit unnecessary references to some of
his literary parents as well. Though he does allow a line of
Shakespeare's to join in his song, Williams crossed out extra
lines and a reference to Shakespeare in an early version of
"Asphodel."[5] In the finished poem Williams asks Flossie and
the reader to imagine "a field made up of women / all silver-
white"; in the earlier version Williams lets us see too much of
the background materials of his imagination. Those silvery
women are "all pied as Shakespeare saw them / where ladies
smocks / were silver white." Williams deleted this extra material; in the final version he does his own seeing. Williams decided to condense and to suggest, relying on the impact of the
single image.

    A reference to Keats is more oblique in Williams' work-

    5. *PB*, 170, ll. 8 and 9, are a syncopated version of Shakespeare's opening
lines from "Song of Spring," *Love's Labour's Lost*. *Shakespeare's Songs and
Poems*, ed. Edward Hubles (New York, 1959), 181.

sheets for Section II, where he uses this passage as a preface to talking about the bomb:

> We are like gnats
>   flying near the water.
>   that do not
> aspire even to a sparrow's view
>   of the sky.

The passage recalls the last stanza of Keats' "To Autumn."[6] Williams chose to leave out this passage, which sounded bitter and overly pessimistic; at this moment in the poem he seemed to be writing himself into a state of gloom. The final version does acknowledge our capacity for self-destruction, but the tone of the poem is one of hopefulness. We are watching Williams consider the arrangement of the parts of his poem. He saves his comments on the bomb until several pages later in the section, so that the reader is not overwhelmed by his message.

By cutting this section, Williams took back the poem from his earliest poetic source. In the final version of Section II Williams begins by "approaching" his own death, making a very personal statement.

Several other important deletions appear to have been made not only for tone and clarity, but also for appropriate content. In the worksheets, Williams compares himself to Homer a few more times than he does in the final version of "Asphodel." The worksheet passages may be seen as merely repetitive and therefore best deleted for the sake of sharpness, bareness of line. But the comparisons to Homer might also strike the reader as too arrogant. It is important for Williams to sound calm and resolved, wise, in the final version. For Williams to have called attention to his wisdom would have drawn attention away from the music and the poet's assertions of love. For him to have expressed doubts and questions within the poem, more vulnerability than he shows, would have detracted from

6. John Keats, "To Autumn," esp. ll. 27–33; "Then in a wailful choir the small gnats mourn," etc., in M. H. Abrams (ed.), *Norton Anthology of English Literature* (2 vols.; New York, 1962), II, 395.

the tone of the resolve and joy that finally dominates the poem. So we may be glad that Williams left out the following comparisons and questions to himself, though we may be interested in the questions. This passage begins after Williams sees the man in the subway who reminds him of his father (Book III); in the worksheet he says, "I saw in that man / all men, myself." Then he goes on to ask,

<blockquote>

                  Is this irrelevant
to my story?
         Or will it save me
                 from my sorrow?
I do not think so.
         Odysseus did not think so
            or Homer. . . .

</blockquote>

The poet is asking himself if art can really save him from sorrow, or from death. In the rough-draft version the poet adds, "We are on our own / to make our own." Perhaps this insight into his aloneness and individuality, responsibility, led him to leave out this and other references to Homer.

In the worksheets Williams emphasizes the theme of "old men" and of "blindness"—so much so that the poem becomes depressing at times. The one or two references in the final version are enough for us to understand that Williams is at a late stage in life, that he identifies with the "blind old man" and "sexless old man," Homer, whose bones are part of the sea (*PB*, 160). We may be glad that Williams left out this passage:

<blockquote>

These things are opposed
         to the present monomania of the world:
               old men
because they are sterile
         and among them
               have been singers
that are remembered.

</blockquote>

Williams talks about how the old man's work "summerizes" or summarizes the complexities of his experience:

<blockquote>

               . . . a young man
is all false starts.

</blockquote>

> He does not finish
> anything. He has
> no center from which to start.
> A garden,
> which the old men love to tend
> summerizes the mind
> with its variety.

Williams left his opinions out of the poem, and merely suggested them, leaving the reader to experience the mood of the older man's wisdom that radiates from a center.

A page that Williams crossed out completely with a large X concerns itself with "life after death."

> It is perhaps fanciful
> to speak of the life after death
> but this is true of it
> that it is flowerlike
> in that the flowerlike itself
> is mortal.

The poem goes on to say, somewhat mysteriously, that

> . . . The product
> of the flame is the rose
> and all the lesser flowers;
> melting worlds
> cannot escape it
> in the end.

Perhaps Williams left out this passage because it was too speculative; the sound of "life after death" would remind the reader of religion, and Williams cut from the final version overt references to religion.

Furthermore, the passage about life after death is esoteric with its talk of the flame and the rose. The rose in this passage would seem to be "mortal" and hence subject to "melting worlds" of death "in the end." Perhaps Williams was not certain that he believed this idea to be true, for "Asphodel" appears to be a statement of art's staying power; the flower seen through the imagination defies "melting worlds." Possibly Williams cut this passage because he found himself sounding a bit like Eliot. It is impossible to tell for sure why Williams chose to cut this, but the passage is atypical, complex and obscure. In his better judgment, Williams decided to stick to matters at hand, to the memories evoked by a particular flower and a particular woman.

Some long sections that are left out of the final version are merely "talky," cranked out of the triadic line. Williams seems to be "talking on" about the interconnection of the flower and the poetic image, rather than establishing equivalents. He explores the ramifications of the association of flower and image rather than the suggestive power of the connection. The prose in the long, explanatory passages becomes stiff and didactic. The triadic line has the effect of sounding like creaky bones rather than the flowing of a river.

> And poems I say are flowers
> and have the characteristics
> of flowers:
> they are rooted
> and spring each from its own root
> unvarying
> but they are rooted
> also in the mind and the heart,
> until the heart fail.

And so we would have learned the characteristics of flowers, and that their strength fails with "heart failure." This bit of grim comedy, unintended no doubt, was best left out. In the final version, the flower, the image pressed by the imagination, triumphs.

Williams includes some interesting ideas on the special, privileged view of the flowers in hell in his "lecture" on the life and role of flowers in art. He returns to the theme of "seeking a soil," a phrase we might associate with Williams' interest in finding the "American idiom." But this material is best left to the essays and suggested, not outlined, in a poem. The rough-draft sheet (marked 10) contains this account, left out in the final version:

> This is the secret
> of all flowers: they are born

```
to seek a soil
            to which they are native
                        and upon which
        they thrive even if
                    they have to go to hell
                                for it. But they will
            nonetheless,
                        if they are loved,
                                curiously,
   being poets,
   conduct  those who shelter them
                        to a view
                                which no one else
            ^
                    can afford. . . .
```

In the worksheet version, "to which they are native" is crossed out; "being poets, conduct" is added on in pencil on one margin; "can afford" is also added in pencil. From this account we learn that flowers, poets like Williams, will obtain for those who love them a costly and rare view of hell. In the final published version Williams says nothing about the flowers going down to hell. He speaks from his own point of view, with integrity; he does not identify with flowers but speaks of his own fate.

```
I cannot say
            that I have gone to hell
                        for your love
    but often
                found myself there
                            in your pursuit.
    I do not like it
                and wanted to be
                        in heaven.  (PB, 156).
```

Williams tried a version of Section III that was not included in the final poem. This section, beginning "We shall not live forever . . . ," contains passages that seem to add music, to have a sense of unity to them. Of the sea and of gardens Williams sings,

```
It is all one
                with the timelessness
    of the Iliad
```

               or the fugal music
                      of Bach.
       If you would be remembered
              to the rose
                      add the timelessness
of the sea
              and you have the rhythm:
                      a rose, is a rose,
is a rose, is a rose
              in perpetuity
                      I is the river
of heaven
              which in the end
                      absorbs all or lives.

I have left the spelling as Williams typed it, though "I is the river" must have been a slip and meant to be read as "It is the river." In this passage we find a statement of the continuity and unity of things of beauty through rhythm, through the music created by the poets. Music itself is the "river of heaven" that transposes the poet outside of time. This page and the other four in the set, though they contain interesting and perhaps usable content for "Asphodel," were left out of the final version. The emphasis on Book III in the published version is on forgiveness and on Williams' sad encounter (or lack of encounter) with the man who reminds him of his father. Williams must have decided that these themes were more central to his purpose in his love song than the statement about *The Iliad* and Bach, with its emphasis on art. The theme of communication is made personal as well as universal in the published version of Book III, for the reader is shown scenes from the poet's life which the poet uses to call for renewed communication.

The poet not only deletes material to cut and sharpen his final version, but he also adds words to create subtlety and to add to the atmosphere of intimacy. On page 2 of what appears to be the third attempt to work at Book I, Williams changes "Of love, abiding love, / it will be singing" to "Of love, abiding love, / it will be telling." "Telling" has a more serious tone in this context. Furthermore, the poet lets us know that there is

a narrative strain to his poem. On the same page the poet
adds the word "wholly" in pencil to the stanza:

> tho' too weak a wash of crimson
> colors it   wholly
> to make it ∧ credible

"Wholly" is a word that adds subtle modulations to the meaning. Without "wholly" we are left to understand that the weakness of the poet's passion belies the story he wishes to tell. But
"wholly credible" leaves us more room to listen, to doubt the
poet's sincerity somewhat, to admire his artistry and will to
love the more. In one of the earliest versions Williams included and then crossed out the word "yet" ("to make it yet
credible"), helping us to understand that he did intend to
build an argument on his own behalf, to work so skillfully in
his poem that Flossie and the reader would eventually have to
believe him. The omission of "yet" allows the poet more stra-
tegic subtlety in his final version.

On the page marked "3" of this same set the poet adds
"forebodingly" to modify the nature of Asphodel's presence
in his boyhood collection:

> I had a good collection
> The asphodel
>   FOREBODINGLY
> was ∧ among them.

Without "forebodingly" the statement about the asphodel's
being a part of the collection is a neutral statement of fact. The
word makes the reader think more about the nature of this
flower that has suddenly become more strange. The word
adds a mood of intrigue, involving the reader who must continue on to find what it is about this flower that bodes ill.

In one place Williams adds punctuation that adds drama to
the scene in the subway where the poet sees a man who re-
sembles his father. One version on the page reads,

> I remember
> when my father was a young man—
> I saw it in a photograph

> he wore such a beard.
> He reminds me
> of my father.

Williams then crosses out the first line on the page "I remember" and adds in penciled hand, "Then I remembered!" The change in tense and the addition of the exclamation point has the effect of conveying the poet's excitement and allowing the reader to share in the experience of discovery, of memory. Williams crossed out "he" and changed the phrase to "This man reminds me" to make the situation more concrete and particular.

On the first draft of Book I, marked "for Flossie," Williams added in pencil "together" to the phrase "We've had a long life." The effect of "together" adds to the sense of shared experience. On this same page the poet changed ". . . as their eyes fill / with tears" to "as our eyes fill / with tears," thereby making his wife and himself partners in seeing. In the margin, by this line, Williams added in pencil "intimately" as if to remind himself to add music of intimacy. Crafty Odysseus!

Throughout the rough-draft version we find notes typed into the poem, and there are occasional handwritten notes, which allow us to share the poet's struggle for a "redeeming language."

Among the typed passages in the worksheets we find instances where Williams seems actually to be struggling with memory loss. We are reminded that the poet's stroke had caused a state of partial memory loss, and something of the problem shows up in the typing. At the bottom of a page marked 23 the poet sounds as if he is struggling to be clear.

> He fought for the
> Resistance during the recent war
> We forget
> I begin to forget.
> Where are you?
> In heaven?
> Is it the other side
> of where I find myself?

In this reference to the Resistance and to the war, Williams is calling upon his memory of René Char, whom he admired and had translated.[7] The poet wonders about Char's death, since he too is facing death, since he "often finds himself in hell." Has René Char fared better?

In such passages we seem to be watching the poet speaking to himself, groping for his memories. His questions are moving, private ones. Fighting against the limitations imposed by his recent illness, memory *is* "an accomplishment."

The handwritten notes on page 2 of the second attempt at a draft of Book I are revealing of the poet's purpose and state of mind when writing the poem. At the top of the page, which begins "Love alone / stays, to which the appeal," the poet has written in handscript, "pleading for us who are subject to death's blows." Surely we could not find a more direct statement of the poet's purpose. On the same page he types "But give me time" and adds in handscript, "To make sure." Williams desperately hoped to make himself understood. But to whom does one appeal against "death's blows"? To love, which "alone stays"? To Flossie? To the poem itself? Language does speak to itself in lyric poetry, it becomes its own hearing, though the poet hopes there will be many listeners.

In the final version Williams just asks for time. Perhaps Williams realized he could not be "sure" of winning in his struggle, or perhaps by the end of "Asphodel" he had found a sureness and sense of resolve.

In the middle of the page the typed lines read, "The roses fill the garden with their perfume / a whirling / presence bewilders me." Then Williams writes in by hand, "am bewildered. —half awake I plead for time." Crossed out are the words "I cannot do it at once," indicating Williams' impatience about saying what he needs to say quickly, almost simultaneously, indicating his recognition that he must be patient and let the story unfold. We seem to be reading a journal

7. René Char, *Hypnos Waking and Prose by René Char* (New York, 1956), contains two translations by William Carlos Williams, 252–53.

of the poet's notes to himself of his feelings about his materials, which include many fears. The last eight lines on the page are crossed out; we can read "The word's way / is the flower's way in the wood" through the pencil mark. At the bottom of the page Williams writes, in handscript, "Near something but I am not sure." So we see that the poet was discovering much of his material as he went along. The triadic line provided him with the order that he needed to take risks.

Williams' handwritten notes on "Asphodel" give us a glimpse of what the flower stood for to him. The words are not all decipherable, but what is clearly readable says:

> of asphodel that greeny flower
> wet with morning dew
> Thou cast up a memory.
> (in spite of lightning)
> that through all *defeats*
> (it still warms me
> + barely ruddies) faintly ruddies
> *and* cheers   my
> *darkest hours, that will come*[8]

This much, at least, is readable. On the page the word "through" is crossed out; the "est" on dark has been crossed out (changing "darkest" to "dark"); and "That will come" has been crossed out. Again we are privileged to witness the poet in the process of talking to himself, of beginning to sound out for himself what the image of asphodel must mean. The poet is planning for an image that will cheer him in the darkness to come. Williams knew that his strokes would come on again and would become progressively more serious.

We find amid the worksheets a handwritten page marked "3" and an attached typed page; both contain notes on the flower asphodel. Williams seems to be defining for himself the suggestions that the flower holds. On the handwritten page the poet writes,

> Of asphodel without
> color, a sort of buttercup

8. This passage is on the front of the hotel menu dated 1952. YALC.

```
         ragged but a
              flower—a
    stringy, colorless ghost
         a sort of mental
 flower, a sort of
              buttercup
                   ranunculosine
    a rumor of a flower
         like a priest in
              hell
    like a lecture on the
         Lord, a Thomist.
    blossoms in those fields
```

It is intriguing for us to see that Williams thinks of "asphodel" as "ragged," "ghostly," "colorless," and not "greeny" as in the poem, a "mental flower" that has a "moral odor" in the poem. The flower is a flower of memory and imaginative life, not a literal flower. Williams cuts out the references to religion in the final version. It is interesting to see that the poet sees himself as displaced, as a "priest in hell"; that his subject matter of imagination, memory and art is God to him. The reference to Thomism suggests dogmatism to the reader, or a lecture on God, and was left out of the final version. Williams may have realized, sadly, that he could not provide that kind of certainty.

The typed version, attached to the handwritten notes discussed above, adds nothing new except that "green" is penciled into the phrase, so that it reads "a sort of green buttercup." The Latin word has been changed to *ranunculaniae*; Williams must have looked it up. If "asphodel" is primarily a "mental flower" it is also a flower found in nature. Williams keeps his feet on earth.

The remaining notes in handscript are scattered through the worksheets. It is intriguing to read them as part of the poet's personal journal of his work. One handwritten page, which appears to be dated January 10, 1950, reads, "V. The River of Heaven Everything—left over that wasn't done as said—*at ease*." At the bottom of the page the poet writes, "not to be mentioned." Williams was beginning *Paterson IV* and realized he would also have to write *Paterson V*. We are reminded of Williams' letter written in 1951, at a time of difficult recovery, where the poet says that he must now "gather the stray ends of what I have been thinking . . . or quit" (*SL*, 298). The command, *"at ease,"* seems to be the poet's note to calm himself, or perhaps it is a note about the tone he wished to achieve in his poetry. Probably he addressed the caution "not to be mentioned" to himself as well, to remind himself not to "blab" about plans for a poem he may not have been sure he could finish. For years he had said that *Paterson* would have four parts—would his readers welcome another chapter, *Paterson V*?

Williams seems to have been satisfied with his work in 1957, when he added a note to the worksheet folder that says, "June 1, 1957, Paterson V—unpublished material the eternal morning of the word." Though by 1957 Williams knew that "Asphodel" was not a part of *Paterson*, it is primarily the tone of this note that interests us. The reference to "the eternal morning of the word" seems to indicate that Williams felt as Mariani imagined him, in the assertion that Williams "has come out on the other side of the apocalyptic moment."[9]

The last handwritten note from the worksheets to consider is Williams' response to a college editor. The editor of the *Sequoya Quarterly* from St. John's College wrote asking him what had influenced him to write poetry, and asking for a definition of poetry. Williams included a one-sentence response to the letter amid his worksheets for "Asphodel." He wrote, "Poetry along with the other arts represents a man's longing to make one with his fellows through the ages upon a basis which asserts their mutual love for the divine." The statement sums up Williams' definition of poetry and his motive for writing in a clear and direct manner, filled with feeling.

9. Paul Mariani, "The Eighth Day of Creation: William Carlos Williams' Late Poems," *Twentieth Century Literature*, XXI (October, 1975), 307.

Index

162 / *Index*

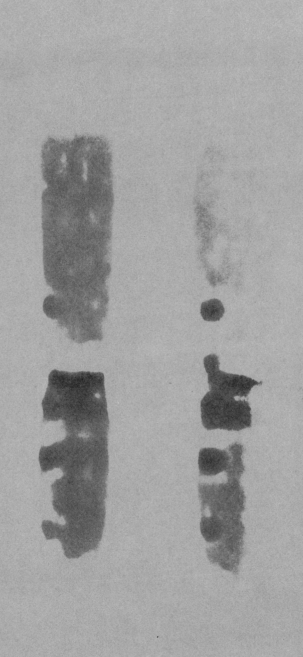